Pivot or Pirouette?

TURNING POINT
ELECTIONS

General Editors: Gerald Baier and R. Kenneth Carty

Since Confederation, Canadians have gone to the polls over forty times in general elections. Sometimes the ruling party was re-elected, other times the government changed hands, but, more often than not, the country would carry on as if little had happened. However, some elections were different. They stirred up underlying divisions, generated debates, gave rise to influential personalities, and energized and reshaped the electorate – ultimately changing the direction the country would follow. Those elections were "turning points." The volumes in this series tell the stories of these turning point elections, focusing on the players, the issues at stake, the campaigns, and the often surprising outcomes that would fundamentally reshape Canadian politics and society. This is the first volume in the series. For a list of other titles, see the UBC Press website, ubcpress.ca/turning-point-elections.

Pivot or Pirouette?

The 1993 Canadian General Election

TOM FLANAGAN

UBCPress · Vancouver · Toronto

31 30 29 28 27 26 25 24 23 22   5 4 3 2 1

Printed in Canada on FSC-certified ancient-forest-free paper (100% post-consumer recycled) that is processed chlorine- and acid-free.

Library and Archives Canada Cataloguing in Publication

Title: Pivot or pirouette? : the 1993 Canadian general election / Tom Flanagan.

Names: Flanagan, Thomas, author.

Description: Series statement: Turning point elections | Includes bibliographical references and index.

Identifiers: Canadiana (print) 20220265674 | Canadiana (ebook) 20220265690 | ISBN 9780774866835 (softcover) | ISBN 9780774867047 (PDF) | ISBN 9780774867740 (EPUB)

Subjects: LCSH: Canada. Parliament – Elections, 1993. | LCSH: Coalition governments – Canada. | LCSH: Political parties – Canada. | CSH: Canada – Politics and government – 1993-2006.

Classification: LCC JL193 .F53 2022 | DDC 324.971—dc23

Canadä

UBC Press gratefully acknowledges the financial support for our publishing program of the Government of Canada (through the Canada Book Fund), the Canada Council for the Arts, and the British Columbia Arts Council.

UBC Press
The University of British Columbia
2029 West Mall
Vancouver, BC V6T 1Z2
www.ubcpress.ca

Contents

Foreword

Turning Point Elections ... and the Case of 1993

Gerald Baier and R. Kenneth Carty

FREE, COMPETITIVE ELECTIONS are the lifeblood of modern democracies. And nowhere has this been more apparent than in Canada, a country cobbled together by bargaining politicians who then continually remade it over a century and a half by their electoral ambitions, victories, and losses. In a continually changing country, the political parties that emerged to manage this electoral competition also found themselves continually changing as they sought to reflect and shape the country they sought to govern. The stories of these politicians, these parties, and these elections are a critical part of the twists and turns that have produced Canada.

Canadians have now gone to the polls in forty-four national general elections. The rules, participants, personalities, and issues have varied over time, but the central quest has always been the same – the chance to win the right to govern a complex and dynamic country. About twice as often as not, the electorate has stuck with who they know and returned incumbents to the governing mantle. Only about a third of the time have the government's opponents, promising something new or different, been elevated to power. But whatever the outcome over all forty-four elections, the contest has ultimately been between the Liberal and Conservative parties for the top prize. While other challengers have come and gone, and some have even endured, the persistence of the Liberal/Conservative dichotomy has defined the effective bounds of Canada's democratic politics.

More than one hundred years ago, a visiting French observer, André Siegfried, argued that Canadian elections were essentially meaningless because the core two parties were little more than unprincipled reflections of one another, preoccupied only with their continued existence. To the extent this was true, it reflected Canadian politicians' determination to build "big tent" political parties able to appeal to the wide range of discordant regions and interests, religious and language groups, and parochial claims that dominated the country's political life and public conversations. If the Liberal Party dominated national electoral politics over the twentieth century, to become labelled as the country's "natural governing party," it was because its tent was larger and rooted in an overwhelming mastery of Quebec constituencies. And so, a long list of Liberal leaders – Wilfrid Laurier, Mackenzie King, Louis St. Laurent, Pierre Trudeau, Jean Chrétien – kept leading their party back to office election after election. In a country being continually transformed on almost every conceivable dimension, electoral outcomes were remarkably stoic in comparison.

Occasionally, though, conditions allowed for rather abrupt shocks to this seeming political tranquility. There were exceptions to the familiar story of incumbents cruising to victory. In part, those occasions reflected the workings of a first-past-the-post electoral system that was capable of generating both stability and volatility. The difference between hanging on to power or being roundly booted from grace could be just a few percentage points change in a party's support, or a strong showing by one or more third parties bleeding off a portion of one of the big tent party's vote. So some elections were different, thrusting new and exciting personalities to the fore, generating principled debates on fundamental issues, electrifying and engaging the electorate, and reshaping the parties and the dynamics of party competition, all with lasting consequences for the direction of the country to follow. These elections stand out as turning points. The stories of the turning point elections are more than accounts of compelling figures, dramatic campaigns, and new political alignments. They also reveal how the pressures of demographic, socioeconomic, and regional change were challenging the status quo; how they broke the political moulds of previous election contests; and how the turn played out in the politics, policies, and governments of succeeding decades. In each of the turning point elections, we see how the evolving political landscape allowed politicians to crystallize, and often personify, the issues of a distinctive agenda and create a campaign that would mobilize and reshape the complex coalitions of supporters that constituted the nation's political parties. These turning points constituted the starting point for a new and different cycle in the contest between the two great big tent parties that have dominated the struggle for power and office and defined the nature and evolution of Canadian democracy.

THIS ACCOUNT OF the 1993 general election tells the story of one of the country's most dramatic political contests, one whose outcome threatened a century of shared understandings and practices. After decades of predictable, even routine, elections, 1993 produced the greatest electoral earthquake in any democracy during the twentieth century. It saw the two old parties running behind new unproven leaders, one the country's first female prime minister. It saw the rise of two new political parties that threatened the very viability of the country as a coherent national political community. It saw the apparent collapse of an effective social democratic alternative. The result was a fragmented parliament, a government with minority support, and the largest opposition party committed to the break-up of the federation.

As a senior member of the Reform Party team challenging the system, Tom Flanagan was an important player in the story he tells. With a clear eye, he charts the disintegration of the Conservative government that had assembled an oversized coalition of supporters that it inevitably came to disappoint. It was the collapse of that Conservative big tent that provided the space for the emergence of the western Reform and the Bloc Québécois parties, which sought to redefine the very nature and practice of Canadian politics and government. But as Flanagan also notes, it was that same shattering of the Conservative coalition that allowed the Liberals to reclaim their position as the country's natural majority government.

Such a dramatic turn spurred its own set of changes. Given the fragmented cast of the party system, the Liberals went on to easily win the next few elections with a historically low vote share. Having lost control of their historic Quebec base, their long claim to be the only party able to manage the historic political bargain tying French- and English-speaking Canadians together suddenly evaporated, and the party appeared more vulnerable than ever. On the other side of the political spectrum, a series of electoral disappointments stimulated the restructuring of a Conservative Party, albeit one with a more distinctive ideological appeal.

Like Siegfried's account of the country's electoral politics in 1904, this analysis of the 1993 contest reveals much of the essence of Canadian democracy. Flanagan concludes that, despite the unprecedented electoral eruption, the seemingly familiar party system had been completely restored within two decades. As they have for over a century, Liberals and Conservatives again compete for office as two big tent organizations, seeking to gather support from across the country. The dramatic turn of 1993 had changed the personnel, the government, and the parties of the day, but in the longer run, the country's party politics simply pivoted to find a new equilibrium and returned to the distinctive pattern of electoral competition that had long characterized Canadian public life.

Preface

THE 1993 ELECTION is not just an abstract topic of research for me. I was personally involved in the events before, during, and after the ballots were cast and counted. So when Ken Carty, an authority on Canadian political parties, invited me to write a book about the election, I was delighted to accept. It gave me a chance to revisit an important part of my own life.

At Preston Manning's invitation, I went to work for the Reform Party in May 1991. I initially held the title of Director of Policy, Strategy, and Communications, which was later changed to Director of Research to better reflect what I was actually doing. From the beginning, I wasn't entirely happy in my job. I supported Reform's agenda, including better representation for Western Canada, Senate reform, balanced budgets, and opposition to one-sided demands from Quebec for constitutional change. However, I had trouble fitting into Reform's nascent organization. That I had no real experience in partisan politics made things even more difficult.

I left my paid job with Reform at the end of 1992 and was dismissed as an informal adviser in August 1993. At the time, I blamed Manning for the breakdown in our relationship, but now I would say my own inexperience was at fault. Academic life is a poor preparation for high-level participation in politics; it places too much emphasis on being intellectually right and not enough on understanding how to build support for the cause. Anyway, I wrote a book about my experience with Reform titled *Waiting for the Wave: The Reform Party and Preston Manning*. For anyone interested in reading it, I would recommend the second edition, which has a slightly different title and explains how the founding of Reform started the process that led to Stephen Harper's Conservative government.[1]

While still inside the Reform organization, I played some part in shaping the party's campaign against the Charlottetown Accord. That's a major theme in this book because what happened in the 1992 referendum presaged in many ways what happened in the 1993 election. I was out of the Reform organization by the time the election took place, but I did do quite a bit of media commentary during the campaign. At that time, I was the only person in the country with academic credentials who had been on the inside with Reform, so the media called frequently for interviews. Then as now, the media love a source with inside credentials who has had some differences with the leader.

After 1993, I continued to do a lot of media, becoming a columnist for the *Alberta Report,* the *Globe and Mail,* and the *National Post* in that order. I didn't get drawn back into active politics until 2001, when Stephen Harper decided to run for the leadership of the Canadian Alliance, the successor party to Reform. I had gotten to know Harper when we both worked for Reform, and I had remained friendly with him in the intervening years. I ended up managing his successful leadership campaign. Afterwards I worked for a year as chief of staff in the Office of the Leader of the Opposition, then managed Harper's campaign for the leadership of the new Conservative Party of Canada as well as the party's national campaign in the 2004 election.

I relinquished the position of campaign manager to assistant manager Doug Finley, but worked again in the Conservative war room in the 2005–06 campaign. Doug helped bring Stephen Harper and the Conservatives to power in 2006, but he died much too early in 2013, having just been appointed to the Senate. I can't help wondering whether, if Doug had enjoyed better health and could have continued as campaign manager, Harper might have defeated Justin Trudeau and the Liberals in 2015. Rest in peace, Doug. You were a pillar of strength for the whole campaign team.

I wrote another book – it's the disease of professors – about these experiences titled *Harper's Team: Behind the Scenes in the Conservative Rise to Power.*[2] Because of my work with Harper, the Canadian Alliance, and the Conservative Party of Canada, I had a fruitful vantage point for observing national politics for five crucial years leading up to the Conservative Party's first government in 2006. I mention that first government here because it was an important part of the aftermath of 1993. That earlier election had left a lot of unfinished business, and I had the privilege of helping finish some of it.

Thus, the election of 1993 is not just an abstract research topic to me. I was engaged in the events before, during, and after – sometimes on the periphery, sometimes at the centre. For about fifteen years, much of my professional life was taken up with planning strategy and managing campaigns for the Reform Party, the Canadian Alliance, and the Conservative Party of Canada. When I wasn't actively engaged in partisan politics, I was talking and writing about the events. They are as vividly alive to me now as they were then, although I hope time has made my judgment more balanced and fair.

Thus, the reader will notice that I speak with different voices at different points in the book. For the most part, it is straightforward political history – the story of the 1993 election, what led up to it, and what happened as a result of it. But there is no story without a perspective. There has to be a point of view to determine what is relevant among an infinite number of facts, and to weave them together into a coherent account. For me, that unifying perspective comes from my academic discipline of political science, particularly the subfield known as rational choice.

As will be explained later in more detail, rational choice assumes that all human beings are self-interested and that politics is an arena in which they pursue self-interest through the building of coalitions with others. Coalition theory and the median voter model of partisan choice are the intellectual foundation of this book. Coalition theory is dominant in explaining the crack-up of Brian Mulroney's Conservative party in 1992–93, and the median voter model helps explain the course that federal politics took after 1993. I will explain each at the appropriate time; apart from that, I won't go into the other branches of rational choice except to mention some further titles in the Suggestions for Further Reading.

I should also mention that my view of coalitions is bolstered by contemporary developments in evolutionary biology, particularly in the subfield of primatology. Decades of scientific research have taught us that human beings are not the only primate species to engage in politics, if by that we mean a competitive struggle for rank in society. We humans, as well as our chimpanzee and bonobo cousins, conduct that struggle by forming supportive coalitions to attain dominance. Without belabouring the point, I will bring in some findings from primatology to bolster the interpretation of coalitions – including both their formation and disintegration – in Canadian politics.

Then there is my voice as a participant, recalling important, interesting, or illustrative events in which I happened to be involved. I leaven the story with personal anecdotes where I think they may help the reader's understanding. I try to be fair to leaders such as Joe Clark, Brian Mulroney, Kim Campbell, Jean Chrétien, Paul

Martin, Jack Layton, Lucien Bouchard, and Gilles Duceppe, as well as the staffers who worked for them and the voters who supported them. They were opponents, to be sure, but with the passage of time, I can see that we were all players in a play without a playwright. We improvised as we went along, all working for what we thought was best but no one knowing for sure what that might be. As the poet T.S. Eliot said of the human condition in *Four Quartets:* "For us, there is only the trying."[3]

Leaders of political parties play central roles in elections, and most voters know a fair bit about them when the election is held. But by the time anyone reads this book, thirty years will have elapsed since 1993. The political leaders whose names were household words then may be only dimly remembered, or perhaps completely forgotten, in today's world, so let me say a little about them to help the contemporary reader follow the story.

A couple of leaders I knew quite well, I had casual contact with a few, and I came to know others by reading about them. From what I now know of all these leaders, they were outstanding people. Like other human beings, they had flaws and made mistakes, but they were all highly intelligent, hardworking, dedicated patriots (Bouchard and Duceppe were Quebec rather than Canadian patriots, but the point remains valid). That generation of leaders can take credit for some remarkable achievements. To mention only a few:

- Joe Clark defeated the seemingly invincible Pierre Trudeau in the 1979 election.
- Brian Mulroney built a political grand coalition, based above all on a profound realignment of the political sympathies of Quebecers, especially francophones.
- Preston Manning founded a successful new party that came to dominate an entire region of Canada.
- Audrey McLaughlin and Kim Campbell became the first female leaders of major political parties.

- Kim Campbell was the first woman to become prime minister of Canada.
- Jean Chrétien rose from seeming political oblivion to become a long-serving prime minister.
- Paul Martin is often considered the most successful finance minister in Canadian history for taming the federal deficit and putting the Canada Pension Plan on a sound financial footing.
- Lucien Bouchard founded a dynamic new party and almost took Quebec to independence.
- Gilles Duceppe made Bouchard's party a going concern for several more elections after its founder left for provincial politics.
- Stephen Harper pulled off a merger of the Canadian Alliance with the Progressive Conservatives and parlayed that into almost ten years as prime minister.
- Jack Layton rebuilt the New Democratic Party and led it to unprecedented heights as official opposition in 2011.

Of course, one could just as easily make a list of these leaders' notorious failures:

- Joe Clark fumbled away his 1979 victory, paving the way for Pierre Trudeau's return to power.
- Brian Mulroney's grand coalition broke up and he ended as perhaps the most unpopular prime minister in Canadian history.
- Preston Manning's Reform Party could never break out of its Western heartland, and Reformers ended by abandoning his leadership for that of Stockwell Day.
- Lucien Bouchard never achieved independence for Quebec.
- Gilles Duceppe and the Bloc Québécois were repudiated by Quebec voters in 2011.
- After becoming leaders, both Audrey McLaughlin and Kim Campbell led their parties to devastating defeats in 1993.

- After winning three majority governments in a row, Jean Chrétien was forced out of the Liberal leadership by his old rival Paul Martin.

- After achieving his lifelong ambition to become prime minister, Paul Martin served less than two years before losing to Stephen Harper's Conservatives.

- Stephen Harper was defeated in 2015 and his dream of making the Conservatives the new majority party seems stalled, if not dead.

- Jack Layton's great success of 2011 did not survive his untimely death, and the NDP is now back to its historical position as a third party with no realistic chance of forming a government.

One of my first academic papers, published in 1972, was on the importance of Fortuna in the political thought of Machiavelli.[4] Fifty years later, we can see how Canadian political leaders rose and fell with the turning of Fortune's wheel.

Of course many other people were involved in these events in addition to the leaders of political parties. Appendix 1, "List of Key Players," and Appendix 2, "Timeline of Events," will help readers keep track of these players and how they participated in the run-up to the 1993 election, the election campaign, and the political aftermath.

This UBC Press series is about elections deemed to be "turning points" in Canadian political history. But what is a turning point? Sometimes it means taking off in a new direction, making a 90-degree turn so to speak. For a while that seemed to be the meaning of the 1993 election, which brought a new set of political leaders and two new parties with new leaders and novel agendas to Parliament. And indeed 1993 was clearly a realigning election, as that term is used in political science. Large numbers of voters shifted their allegiance, not just for one moment of deviation but for a much longer term. Yet with the advantage of three decades of hindsight, the turning point now seems more like a pirouette, a 360-degree revolution, after which Canadian politics is back on the same track that it had followed for many decades. To quote T.S. Eliot again: "In my end is my beginning."[5]

And yet another qualification is needed. Throughout Canadian history up to 1993, Quebec had always been the linchpin of federal politics. With exception of a few brief and unstable interludes, the governing party always depended on holding a sizable majority of seats in Quebec. That mould was broken in 1993, when Quebecers gave almost half their votes and a large majority of seats to the Bloc Québécois. Since then, Quebec has never backed either the Liberals or Conservatives in the same overwhelming way that it did from 1867 through 1988.

But if 1993 was as much pirouette as pivot, it was not just a meaningless revolution. It was part of the pattern of Canadian politics, in which the entry of new parties shakes up the customary order of things. New parties are one of the great sources of creativity in Canadian politics; without them, politics would often be a mind-numbing game of inches, in which two big parties struggle for the soul of the median voter. The ideas of the gate-crashers often seem strange and even alarming, but that may be the price of innovation.

Thus 1993 cannot be understood in isolation. It was one of a series of elections that upset the previous equilibrium, bringing new parties, new leaders, and new agendas to the fore. Canada's political history features punctuated equilibrium – occasional dramatic changes at election time followed by the emergence of a new equilibrium incorporating new parties, leaders, and agendas. Properly understood, the election of 1993 was not a one-off disruption; it is an example of events that have happened before and will happen again, as Canada's politics adjust to ever-changing demographic, economic, and social realities.

Pivot or Pirouette?

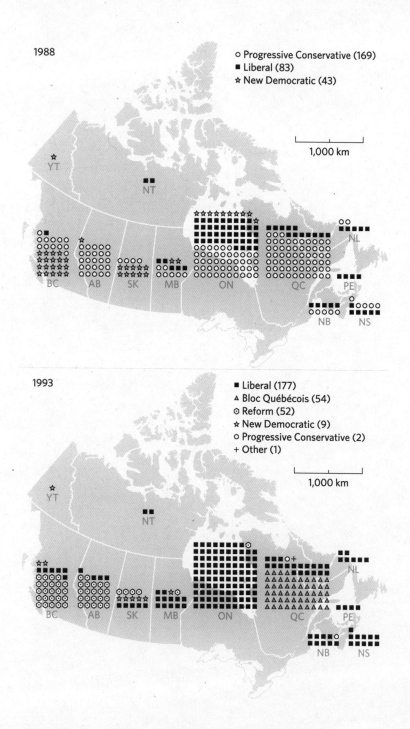

1988

- ○ Progressive Conservative (169)
- ■ Liberal (83)
- ☆ New Democratic (43)

1,000 km

1993

- ■ Liberal (177)
- ▲ Bloc Québécois (54)
- ⊙ Reform (52)
- ☆ New Democratic (9)
- ○ Progressive Conservative (2)
- + Other (1)

1,000 km

Introduction

THE FEDERAL ELECTION of 1993 was in some ways the most peculiar election in Canadian history. To understand its oddity, you have to compare its results with those of the preceding election, held in 1988. The statistical comparison is summarized in Table I.1. First, look at the Progressive Conservatives (PCs). Having won a huge victory in 1984, they were re-elected in 1988 with a plurality of 43 percent of the popular vote and a comfortable majority of 169 out of 295 seats. Admittedly, they were down somewhat from their landslide win of 1984, in which they had taken 211 out of 282 seats, based on 50 percent of the popular vote; but that was a once-in-a-generation landslide, comparable to John Diefenbaker's great victory in 1958.[1] The Conservatives didn't do quite as well in the 1988 election as they had in 1984, but they were still easily in control. Yet in 1993, after Brian Mulroney was succeeded as leader by Kim Campbell, they were reduced to 16 percent of the vote and 2 seats – an unprecedented outcome in Canadian history. The Conservatives had been pummelled before, most notably in 1921, when they fell to third place behind the Liberals and the Progressives, but in that election they still won 49 seats and subsequently became the official opposition when the Progressives declined the honour. The election

TABLE I.1

Canadian general election results, 1988 and 1993

Party	1988		1993	
	% Vote	Seats	% Vote	Seats
Liberal	31.9	83	41.2	177
Progressive Conservative	43.0	169	16.0	2
New Democratic Party	20.4	43	6.9	9
Reform	2.1	0	18.7	52
Bloc Québécois[1]	–	–	13.5	54
Independent[2]	–	–	–	1
Total		295		295

Source: "Canadian Election Results by Party: 1867–2021," https://www.sfu.ca/~aheard/elections/1867-present.html.

1 The Bloc Québécois did not exist in 1988. In 1993, it ran candidates in every Quebec riding but nowhere else.

2 The Independent was Gilles Bernier, formerly the Progressive Conservative MP for Beauce. He was not allowed to run for the PCs in 1993 because of fraud allegations, which were subsequently dismissed. His son, Maxime Bernier, later won the same riding and became prominent in Conservative politics, but left the party after losing the 2017 leadership race to Andrew Scheer.

of 1993 was a setback like no other for the Conservatives, or indeed for any major political party in Canada.

To be sure, governing parties had been decimated before in provincial elections. In the provincial election of 1935, the United Farmers of Alberta, which had governed the province for the preceding fifteen years, won no seats at all. Similarly, the New Brunswick Progressive Conservatives, who had been in power for seventeen years, were completely wiped out in the provincial election of 1987. But such a staggering loss had never occurred at the federal level. Canada is so large and diverse that parties facing repudiation at the polls had always been able to find pockets of strength somewhere in the country to keep themselves going. The PC disaster of 1993 was truly unique in the party's loss of support almost everywhere.

Much of the previous Progressive Conservative vote in the West and in rural Ontario went to the upstart Reform Party of Canada, led by Preston Manning, son of former Alberta premier Ernest Manning. Founded in 1987, Reform had contested the 1988 election in the four Western provinces but had garnered only 2 percent of the vote and had not elected anyone to the House of Commons. Its increase in 1993 to 19 percent of the vote and fifty-two seats was nothing short of astonishing.

Perhaps even more astounding was the performance of the Bloc Québécois (BQ), led by Lucien Bouchard, erstwhile friend of Brian Mulroney. The Bloc was founded in 1990–91 by dissatisfied members of the Progressive Conservatives together with a few Liberals. Now it won almost 14 percent of the vote nationally, which doesn't sound like much until one remembers that the Bloc ran candidates only in Quebec, where it received 49 percent of the popular vote. Its electoral concentration in francophone Quebec ridings enabled it to win fifty-four seats, making it the official opposition. Here was another first in Canadian history: "Her Majesty's Loyal Opposition" was anything but loyal; it now consisted of a separatist party dedicated to the breakup of the country.

The New Democratic Party (NDP) also experienced a surprising outcome, but in the opposite direction. In 1988, the New Democrats had achieved their best-ever result, with 20 percent of the vote and forty-three seats. But their leader, Ed Broadbent, resigned afterwards because he had fallen short of expectations. Pre-election polling had suggested that the NDP might win more seats than the Liberals and replace them as the official opposition. But then the NDP replaced Broadbent with Yukon MP Audrey McLaughlin, giving her the distinction of becoming the first woman to lead a major federal party. Unfortunately for the NDP, her leadership didn't help the party, which in 1993 was reduced to 7 percent of the vote and nine seats – three short of the twelve required for official party status.[2] Being a recognized party with twelve seats in the House of Commons may not sound like much, but it is of considerable practical significance. It gives the party's MPs the right to ask questions in Question Period, to have seats on committees, and to get extra money for research and salaries. Falling below twelve seats is a serious loss.

In 1993, only the Liberals performed more or less according to historical norms. In 1988, they had received 32 percent of the vote and won 83 seats – not a great result, but an improvement over 1984, and good enough to remain the official opposition. Like the NDP, they felt they needed a new leader, and replaced John Turner with Jean Chrétien, who led them to 177 seats based on 41 percent of the vote in the 1993 election, which was enough for a majority government. The Liberals thus continued the tradition they had set since Confederation, becoming the government or official opposition in every election.

In one respect, however, the Liberal performance was unprecedented. In the past, their federal victories had always been anchored by winning a large majority of seats in Quebec, whereas this time they won only 19 of 75 seats in *la belle province.* The Liberals built their majority by taking 98 of 99 seats in Ontario and 31 of 32 in the four Atlantic provinces – also unheard-of results. So from a distance the Liberal victory looked like past triumphs, but a closer view revealed a different configuration of support.

As we will see in more detail later on, the changes in parties' fortunes were magnified by Canada's first-past-the-post (FPTP) electoral system, which can turn small or moderate changes in vote totals into major changes in seats. FPTP helped Reform and the BQ, whose support was concentrated in specific areas, and hurt the PCs and the NDP, whose support in 1993 was much more diffuse. The Liberals, having significant support almost everywhere, were positioned to do the best under the rules of FPTP. Ever since a seminal article by Alan Cairns in the very first issue of the *Canadian Journal of Political Science,*[3] political scientists have emphasized the impact of FPTP upon Canadian politics, and that impact was never more obvious than in 1993.

The Liberals won twenty of thirty-six elections held between 1867 and 1993, while the Conservatives won the other sixteen.[4] That seems fairly even, but most of the Conservative victories lay in the remote past. The Liberals had been dominant since the end of the First World War, winning fifteen elections against eight for the Conservatives. So if you emphasized the Liberals' result, you could say that 1993 was a pretty typical Canadian election. The Liberals, after nine years as official opposition, were restored to government, and in fact would remain in government until 2006, when they would be replaced by a reconstituted Conservative Party. So 1993 was no big deal. *Plus ça change, plus c'est la même chose.*

But below the level of government, the 1993 election was a political earthquake. The Liberals came to power in 1993 without regaining the Quebec base they had lost in 1984 – the first time in Canadian history that the Liberals had won a national election without also winning the majority of seats in Quebec. A brand-new party, based only in Quebec and committed to the independence of that province, was now the official opposition. Reform, another new party, which had held only one seat going into the election (based on a 1989 by-election), had won fifty-two seats, all in the West except one in rural Ontario. And the NDP had been reduced to a fringe player in the House of Commons.

It was a challenge to the prevailing views of Canadian political scientists and journalists. They had seen the Liberals, the PCs, and to a lesser extent the NDP as brokerage parties, devoted to forming national electoral coalitions based on support in every region of the country, with the goal of maintaining national unity.[5] True, the Liberals had been weak in the West for decades, and the PCs and NDP had been weak in Quebec, but all three parties made some effort to build support everywhere, nominating candidates in all ridings in the country.

Now the classic brokerage system, said to be vital to national unity, was threatened by upstart regional parties. Reform did not nominate any candidates in Quebec and was a serious player only in the West, where it won a majority of seats. The Bloc ran candidates only in Quebec and was a serious factor only in majority francophone areas, where it won almost every seat – enough to dominate the province. Reform's leader said he wanted a national party with a Western base, but that was highly aspirational in 1993, when Reform seemed typecast as a Western party. The BQ, for its part, did not even aspire to become a national brokerage party. Its nationalist message of independence for Quebec was meant to appeal only to francophone Québécois and the small number of anglophone and allophone Quebecers who sympathized with Québécois nationalism.

In a later chapter, we will discuss the dynamics of the 1993 election campaign. They were interesting, to be sure, and help to explain the precise shape of the outcome. Campaigns do matter – a lot. But the unprecedented results of the 1993 election were heavily affected by developments that took place years before the election was even called. We must look at some political history before turning to the actual campaign.

Academic life isn't very funny most of the time, so enjoy this joke about university life: A history student delivers his first presentation in a graduate seminar. Afterwards he asks the professor, "How did I do?" "Not bad," answers the teacher, "but remember this is a history course and you have to give more background." A few weeks pass, and then it's time for the student to make his next presentation. He opens by saying, "Slowly the earth cooled." We don't need to go back to the cooling of the earth to understand the 1993 election, but we do need to go surprisingly far back in Canadian history.

Then, after looking at the background to 1993 and the dynamics of the campaign, we have to look at the aftermath. The new parties were now major players in Parliament and Canadian politics generally. Reform played an important role in pushing the Liberals to avoid a debt crisis in 1995, leading to an emphasis on balanced budgets and restraint on federal government spending that lasted for twenty years, until the Liberals returned to power in 2015 under Justin Trudeau's leadership and deficit spending again became the norm.

The BQ exerted influence in a different direction, pushing for the independence of Quebec. Together with its provincial counterpart, the Parti Québécois, the BQ led the charge in the 1995 referendum on Quebec sovereignty. It was a close call for Canada, with the Remain side winning by only 1.2 percentage points. After that, the Bloc settled back into being a regional party representing the interests of Quebec, especially francophone Quebec.

Meanwhile, the Reform Party was also absorbed back into the system. Unlike the BQ, which ran candidates only in Quebec, the Reform Party was driven by a desire to win national elections. It thus transformed itself into the Canadian Alliance and then merged with the remnants of the Progressive Conservatives to become the Conservative Party of Canada, which, led by Stephen Harper, won the elections of 2006, 2008, and 2011 before losing to Justin Trudeau and the Liberals in 2015. The NDP had a star turn as official opposition after the 2011 election but has now fallen back to its accustomed position of a small party exercising influence but not seriously contesting for government (although a confidence-and-supply agreement with the Liberals in 2022 made it a junior partner in government).

Ken Carty, Lisa Young, and William Cross went so far as to say that 1993 saw the birth of a whole new "party system," in which regionally based parties now upstaged the brokerage parties.[6] However, such a diagnosis could be confirmed or disproved only with the passage of time. Indeed, their view seemed to be accurate for a decade, until Reform's successor, the Canadian Alliance, merged with the remnants of the Progressive Conservatives. The merger re-established something that looked very much like the old competition between the Liberals and the Conservatives as parties of government, and the NDP as a party of influence in third place, except that the BQ continued to dominate Quebec.

Apart from the existence of the Bloc Québécois, Canadian politics is now back to more or less where it was before 1984, except that the Liberals no longer have Quebec as a dependable base. The Liberals and a remodelled Conservative Party contest for government, with the outcome depending mainly on who gets the upper hand in Ontario, and to a lesser extent in Atlantic Canada, while the NDP pushes the system from the left without serious expectations of actually governing.

So was 1993 a turning point or a pirouette? It all depends on how long-term your frame of reference is. In the short run, it was a dramatic turning point, producing a Parliament unlike anything Canadians had ever seen, including a separatist party from Quebec and a populist party of the right from Western Canada. But in the longer run, from 1993 to the present, it might be considered an interesting blip that hardly disturbed the sedate course of Canadian political history. Over time, did the turning point turn into a pirouette? We'll take up that question again after looking in more detail at the aftermath of 1993.

1

Grand Coalition

DEMOCRATIC POLITICS CENTRES on building coalitions to win elections and get control of the government.[1] Historically, many philosophers have thought of politics as a distinctively human activity, but modern scientific research has shown that we share a lot of our political behaviour with our primate cousins, especially chimpanzees. A brief look at primate politics will help us understand much of what took place before, during, and after the 1993 election.

The groundbreaking work in this field was *Chimpanzee Politics*,[2] based on the doctoral dissertation of Frans de Waal, now a world-famous primatologist at Emory University in Atlanta, Georgia. Carrying out years of careful observation of chimpanzees at the Arnhem Zoo in the Netherlands, de Waal showed that adult male chimpanzees compete for rank – to be alpha, beta, gamma, and so on down the line. The reward of higher rank consists of more frequent opportunities to copulate with mature females in estrus, thereby leaving more descendants. Of course, chimpanzees may not consciously think about this competition in analytical terms, but evolutionary pressure leads them to act as if they understood the process.

Male chimpanzees vary somewhat but not dramatically in size and strength, so two males acting together can generally defeat another in a fight. This means that the only path to becoming an alpha chimpanzee lies in building a reliable supportive coalition. If alpha, beta, and gamma males stick together, they can guarantee their positions and reap the benefits that come with rank. Such fighting coalitions, reinforced by mutual grooming and occasional food sharing, can last for years, but they suffer from an inherent instability. Being gamma is good, but beta is better, and alpha is best. Thus there is always an incentive for gamma and beta individuals to move up in rank through an attempt to overthrow the alpha individual.

What does this have to do with human politics? Almost everything. For an example, just think of Stephen Harper (beta), Gilles Duceppe (gamma), and Jack Layton (delta) ganging up to defeat Paul Martin (alpha) in the House of Commons, forcing an election in late 2005 in hopes of improving their position in the House of Commons. In the ensuing election, the NDP and Conservatives improved their seat totals substantially and Harper became the new prime minister (alpha). The Liberals lost seats, and Paul Martin resigned as leader, leaving the field entirely like an aging chimpanzee male no longer able and willing to compete for rank. The BQ stayed about the same, losing a couple of seats but retaining its gamma position. Overall, Harper was the big winner, moving from beta to alpha, but Layton also made substantial gains towards rebuilding the NDP and making it a party that could contend for the beta position of official opposition or even the alpha position of government.

Chimpanzees, along with their bonobo cousins, are human beings' closest relatives. Having diverged from the chimpanzee line perhaps six to eight million years ago, we humans have inherited certain patterns of behaviour from our common ancestors, including competition for rank and the formation of coalitions in order to achieve it. There are, however, two key differences between human and chimpanzee politics. First, human intelligence and symbolic communication enable us to form much larger societies than chimpanzee troops numbering a few dozen at most. In these larger human societies, the struggle for rank can lead to the clash of competing coalitions, whereas in chimpanzee societies there is only one coalition of adult males dominating junior males and women. Second, human females can participate in and lead political coalitions, whereas among chimpanzees the competition for rank is strictly a male affair and all males dominate all females. In this respect, the human community is more like the society of our other primate cousins – bonobos – in which females form coalitions to defend themselves from males and sometimes even dominate them.[3]

In modern human societies composed of millions of members, there are at least three types of political coalitions.[4] At the highest level, the leader is surrounded by a tight coterie of advisers and enforcers, all known to each other in a personal way. Then there is the political party as a whole, held together not just by face-to-face bonds but by a belief system (ideology) and a desire for preferment and material benefit (patronage). And finally there is the mass electoral coalition, numbering millions of people who do not know each other at all and who cannot expect individual rewards from the leadership. Their coalitional commitment is tenuous but indispensable; it amounts merely to casting a ballot at the right time for their preferred set of representatives. Electoral coalitions are held together by a sense that their team, if it comes to power, will do things (enact policies) that will benefit people like them. Such beliefs are usually formulated in terms of pursuing a wider public interest, but people inevitably perceive the public interest through the lens of what is good for themselves and for people like themselves.

To summarize in more formal terms, a political coalition is a group of people who act together to achieve benefits for members of the in-group at the expense of those who are excluded. The motor of democratic politics is the competitive struggle of leaders to build winning coalitions providing material and psychic benefits to their supporters.

The Importance of Quebec

A common observation about democratic politics is that minorities who feel threatened or disadvantaged tend to join mass electoral coalitions by engaging in bloc voting. It's a natural human reaction for minorities to cluster their votes around representatives whom they trust to defend their interests. Leaders play to this tendency by emphasizing how the numerical majority threatens members of the minority. Such minority electoral coalitions are extremely important in politics because, if they are large enough and if they are allied with voters elsewhere in the polity, they can be the stable basis of winning coalitions. American examples that Canadian readers will recognize include the contemporary voting behaviour of African Americans (about 80–90 percent Democratic) and the similar Democratic loyalty of white Southerners after losing the Civil War (the "solid South").

The most important example in Canadian political history is the voting behaviour of French Canadians in Quebec, who, though a majority in the province, constitute a linguistic and religious minority in Canada and in North America. The status of Roman Catholicism doesn't matter much anymore in Canadian politics, but the minority status of the French language in Canada is as important as ever.

There are, of course, other examples of durable bloc voting in Canadian politics. Albertans have voted overwhelmingly for a party of the right – Progressive Conservative, Social Credit, Reform, Canadian Alliance, and Conservative Party of Canada – ever since John Diefenbaker became Progressive Conservative leader in 1956. The voting pattern reflects a feeling of being under siege from the rest of Canada, due to the province's oil wealth. But even after years of steady growth, Alberta, with 4.4 million residents and 34 out of 338 seats in the House of Commons, is not big enough to be the linchpin of a durable winning coalition. That distinction has always belonged to Quebec.

In the thirty-four elections from 1867 through 1988, the Liberals won a majority of Quebec seats in twenty-six instances, the Conservatives in only eight. Other parties never came out on top; they made significant showings only in 1945 (Bloc Populaire) and 1962–79 (Ralliement des Créditistes). More importantly for our purposes, five of the eight Conservative victories were in the nineteenth century, when Sir John A. Macdonald was the Conservative leader.[5]

The Liberal dominance of Quebec based on francophone bloc voting began developing in 1891, when native son Wilfrid Laurier first led the Liberals in a national election, and really took hold after the First World War. In 1917, in order to gain support for conscription of men for overseas service, Conservative prime minister Robert Borden invited Liberal leader Laurier to form a government of national unity, as had been done in Britain. When Laurier declined, Borden succeeded in attracting some individual Liberals to sit in cabinet, supported by a large number of Liberal backbenchers. This "Union Government" won a large majority of seats in the 1917 election, but fell apart after the end of the war. Its legacy was overwhelming Liberal dominance in Quebec, where conscription for overseas service had been extremely unpopular, which in turn led to Liberal rule in Canada. As Ken Carty has written: "It turns out that the story of Canada's twentieth century is the story of the Liberal Party and its quite remarkable dominance of the country's political life."[6]

The Conservatives won more seats than the Liberals in Quebec only three times in the period from 1891 through 1988. The first instance was in 1958, when Quebec's Union Nationale premier Maurice Duplessis decided to go all out in support of the

Conservatives led by John Diefenbaker. Duplessis, himself a former Conservative, had always favoured the Conservatives in national elections; now he decided to avenge a grudge that he had nourished against the federal Liberals since 1939, when they helped their Quebec cousins defeat his Union Nationale in the provincial election. Using money and his Union Nationale campaign workers, he targeted fifty ridings, and the Conservatives won exactly those fifty constituencies.[7] Unfortunately for the Conservatives, the alliance with the Union Nationale did not endure. The only two subsequent instances when the Conservatives won Quebec were in 1984 and 1988, when Brian Mulroney performed the near-miracle of shifting francophone voters' allegiance en masse from the Liberals to the Conservatives. It was a shift of loyalty, but it was still bloc voting in support of a mass electoral coalition. We shall see below how the miracle was accomplished.

Moreover, until Mulroney worked his magic, the Liberals did not merely dominate Quebec; they virtually *owned* it. Between 1917 and 1980, there were fourteen elections in which the Conservatives won only five or fewer seats in Quebec. In the five elections held after Pierre Trudeau became Liberal leader in 1968, the Conservative seat totals in Quebec were four, three, two, two, and one, respectively.

The key to Canadian politics from 1867 through 1988 was that whoever dominated the francophone vote in Quebec dominated Canada. Only in eight elections out of thirty-four did the party that took fewer seats in Quebec win the overall election and form a government. Four of these were short-lived Conservative minority governments (1925, 1957, 1962, 1979), and two were during the First World War, when the Liberal Party was internally divided over the conscription issue. For all practical purposes, the rule held true: if you controlled the francophone vote, you controlled Quebec; and if you controlled Quebec, you controlled Canada. To quote Carty once more, "Quebec was the lynchpin of the party's successive national electoral victories."[8]

The only question was whether the Liberals or Conservatives would exert control in Quebec. Mostly it was the Liberals. The Conservatives were able to win in Quebec in the nineteenth century only under Macdonald, and in the twentieth century once under Diefenbaker (1958), when Duplessis was in his corner, and twice under Mulroney.

Prior to the selection of Mulroney as their leader in 1983, the Conservatives were perennially frustrated by their inability to win seats in Quebec, even though they were, in effect, the majority party outside Quebec. Look at the record from 1963 through 1980, when the Liberal leaders were Lester Pearson and then Pierre Trudeau. In these seven elections, the Conservatives won more seats than the Liberals outside Quebec every time except 1968, when Trudeaumania swept the nation. Yet the Liberals won so many seats in Quebec that they formed the government every time, except for Joe Clark's short-lived minority government in 1979. Weakness in Quebec was obviously the Conservatives' Achilles heel, and parties that aspire to form government will sooner or later try to deal with such a weakness. Enter Brian Mulroney. The perennial Conservative weakness in Quebec furnished his great opportunity.

The Grand Coalition

Mulroney was born in 1939 in Baie-Comeau, Quebec, a paper-mill town founded by Robert McCormick, publisher of the *Chicago Tribune*. His father was an electrician who worked at the mill. He grew up not just fluent but idiomatic in both French and English, and earned a law degree from Laval University. Active since his teenage years in Progressive Conservative affairs, Mulroney ran for the leadership in 1975–76 but lost to Joe Clark; it was round one of their long rivalry. Mulroney won round two when he defeated Clark for the leadership in 1983. His biggest selling point was a credible claim to be able to lead a breakthrough in Quebec. When he won the leadership at the nominating convention in June 1983, he spoke about "our area of weakness in French Canada, time after time, decade after decade, election after election, depriving the country of prominent Conservatives such as yourselves of serving in government and influencing the course of our history."[9] The Albertan Clark had worked hard to learn French and could speak it reasonably well, albeit with an accent, but history shows there is no substitute for being from Quebec if you want to win votes in that province.

Mulroney was also an overwhelming personality. He could be venal as well as visionary, vindictive as well as generous. Everything he did seemed larger than life. His extraordinary political gifts helped hold together the outsize coalition that he built. I have met former Progressive Conservatives who spoke with reverence about the way he would phone party workers to congratulate them on their or their children's birthdays. Some of them even kept recordings of these calls so they could listen to them over and over.

I never knew Mulroney personally, but I did witness one example of his passion for politics. On May 17, 2005, former Conservative leadership contestant Belinda Stronach made a highly publicized floor-crossing to the Liberals. As Conservative campaign manager, I was in Ottawa, racing frantically to prepare for the election that we had hoped would follow defeat of the Liberal minority government, but Stronach's defection undercut those plans by moving the Liberals closer to a narrow voting majority in the House of Commons. I happened to be in Stephen Harper's office when a phone call came in from Brian Mulroney, and his resonant baritone filled the room. What was remarkable was that Mulroney had suffered from a variety of ailments in the first part of 2005, including a case of hepatitis from which he nearly died. Yet he still found time and energy to buck Harper up over the telephone. Having endured many defections himself, he knew what it was like to be a leader in those circumstances. I had disliked some of Mulroney's policies in past years, but that phone call gave me a new respect for the man.

Ironically, it was Pierre Trudeau who gave Mulroney the opportunity to make good on his promise of electing a government by winning seats in Quebec. Trudeau had been a member of the Co-operative Commonwealth Federation but accepted an invitation to enter federal politics as a Liberal in 1965, and won the Liberal leadership and became prime minister in 1968. He was motivated by a vision of protecting Quebec's French language and culture while also increasing Quebec's influence in the national government. The adoption of official bilingualism at the national level was an early manifestation of that vision. But Trudeau also sought to entrench Quebec's enhanced position in the constitution, and that proved more difficult to achieve. It did not happen until 1982, with the adoption of the Canadian Charter of Rights and Freedoms, which included some guarantees for French language and culture. But the provincial politicians in Quebec – both the Parti Québécois government, led by René Lévesque, and the Liberal opposition – refused to support the Charter, claiming a veto power over constitutional amendments even though that view had been rejected by the Supreme Court of Canada.[10] In the end, Trudeau got his constitutional amendment package ratified with the support of the federal Parliament and nine out of ten provincial governments. It was a great political victory for Trudeau in its day, but the exclusion of Quebec would provide Mulroney with the wedge he needed to break up the hitherto solid coalition of Liberal support in Quebec.

Trudeau and the Liberals had won seventy-four of seventy-five seats in Quebec in 1980, so they thought they represented public opinion in the province, but pushing through the constitutional amendments lit embers of resentment that Mulroney could fan into open flames. The opportunity came during the 1984 election campaign, in which Mulroney squared off against new Liberal leader John Turner. In the French-language leaders' debate held on July 24, Mulroney spoke of the need to "have Quebec's signature on our constitutional agreement, with honour and enthusiasm."[11]

Immediately afterwards, the Conservatives, who had begun far behind in Quebec, climbed rapidly in the polls, especially among francophones. Mulroney was helped by René Lévesque, whose separatist Parti Québécois was in power provincially. Lévesque decided to take *le beau risque* (literally, "the beautiful risk," perhaps better translated as "the tempting chance") of tacitly supporting the Conservatives, believing he was more likely to get constitutional concessions from them than from the Liberals.[12] In the end, the Conservatives won 50 percent of the popular vote in Quebec and fifty-eight of seventy-five seats. It was a remarkable improvement over 1980, when they had won only 13 percent of the vote and one seat in Quebec. Even more remarkably, the Conservatives won a majority of seats in every province and territory, a feat never before accomplished in a Canadian election.[13]

For anyone familiar with Canadian politics, it was an awe-inspiring result. The political science department at the University of Calgary held an election-results-viewing party on the evening of September 4, 1984. Neil Nevitte, now professor of political science at the University of Toronto and a distinguished student of elections and public opinion, called a francophone friend in Quebec to find out what was happening there. You could hear the cheering in the background as Neil's friend said, "We're all Tories now!" Although that incident occurred almost forty years ago, it is still relevant, because it shows how everything in Canadian politics seemed to have been turned upside down.

Mulroney's great triumph in Quebec was matched across Canada. The Conservatives won more votes and seats than the Liberals in every province, collecting 50 percent of the popular vote and 211 of 282 seats. It was one of the greatest landslides in Canadian history, second only to Diefenbaker's phenomenal victory in 1958, when the Conservatives, helped by Duplessis in Quebec, won 208 of 265 seats, with almost 54 percent of the popular vote. Now, however,

Mulroney, like Diefenbaker, had to face the challenge of managing a larger than necessary coalition.

The American political scientist and rational-choice theorist William Riker made a fundamental contribution to political science in his book *The Theory of Political Coalitions* (1982). He argued that political leaders should aim to form a "minimum winning coalition," that is, a group just large enough to control the decision-making system, with a cushion to allow for uncertainty. Riker applied rational-choice theory to the question of how self-interested coalition members will think and behave. If there are more members than necessary in the winning coalition, he argued, there are more supporters to share the spoils of victory, and the per capita share is reduced.[14] Hence supporters of a larger than necessary coalition will have incentives to defect to new coalition partners who offer them a greater share of the rewards.

For simplicity, let's say that Mulroney had constructed a grand coalition. In the strict terms of rational choice, a grand coalition implies the cooperation of all players, but in ordinary political analysis, an overwhelmingly large coalition is often called a grand coalition, even if it does not literally embrace all members. In the real world of politics, as opposed to the abstract world of mathematical models, leaders cannot calibrate the size of their coalitions precisely. Special conditions existed in 1984, because Trudeau's Liberals had offended some Quebecers by imposing constitutional amendments and had enraged the West through the National Energy Program, which transferred oil revenues from Alberta and Saskatchewan to the federal government.

The stated intention of the National Energy Program was to give Canada more control over oil and gas at a time when political strife in the Middle East was driving prices rapidly higher. The Liberal government wanted to cushion consumers against the effect of price shocks caused by international politics rather than by any shortage of resources. But the consequence of protecting consumers was to transfer billions of dollars from the oil-and-gas-producing provinces of the West, particularly Alberta, by setting domestic prices below international prices. And the transfer was neither unforeseen nor undesired:

> Energy minister Marc Lalonde later said the motive was what Albertans had suspected all along: "to transfer wealth from Alberta to Central Canada. The major factor behind the NEP wasn't Canadianization or getting more from the industry or even self-sufficiency. The determinant factor was the fiscal imbalance between the provinces and the federal government."[15]

With Quebec and the West both aroused against the Liberals, the Conservatives overshot the mark, winning 211 seats when the minimum winning coalition would have been 142 (50 percent plus one of 282 Commons seats). That was a surplus of 69 seats, far more than needed to cushion their parliamentary majority against possible defections, deaths, or retirements. With 28 percent of the vote, the Liberals won 40 seats, only 10 more than the NDP. The Liberals became the official opposition, but just barely.

A coalition as large as Mulroney's is impressive but potentially unstable because its great size reduces the per capita benefits that members receive. The challenge is magnified when the coalition is internally stressed by members who have incompatible goals. The American game theorist Robert Axelrod coined the term "minimum *connected* winning coalition" to highlight the problem.[16] Coalitions, he wrote, are costly to build and maintain; they require frequent negotiations between allies to find areas of common ground. The further apart the coalition partners are situated, the less "connected" they are, the more difficult and costly the negotiations become, and the less likely the coalition is to form and endure.

That is why, for example, the Conservatives and the NDP have never been able to cooperate in Parliament to form a government even when between them they had a majority of votes. They have occasionally gotten together to defeat the Liberals on a confidence vote to force an election, but that is as far as their coalition building has ever extended. The reason is that the Liberals are located ideologically between the NDP and the Conservatives; so the NDP, being more "adjacent" to the Liberals, would rather support a Liberal minority government than try to work out a deal with the Conservatives.

The factual situation of Mulroney's grand coalition was different, but the same principles applied. The Conservative caucus after the 1984 election had three main, equal-sized pillars: fifty-eight members from each of Quebec, Ontario, and the four Western provinces. The Quebec members were mainly concerned with winning benefits, particularly constitutional amendments, for their own province. The Western members wanted the repeal of the National Energy Program as soon as possible, plus a more market-oriented approach to economic policy – lower taxes, privatization of Crown corporations, deregulation of the economy, and reduction of federal deficits, which had skyrocketed during the period of Liberal government. Quebec members and Western members weren't necessarily hostile to each other's objectives, but they were preoccupied with their own concerns. Mulroney's task was to hold this volatile mix together, moving on both fronts without making members of either the Quebec pillar or the Western pillar feel their concerns were being ignored. The coalition was weak on connectivity, and it took a political magician like Mulroney in his heyday to hold it together.

The classic danger in such situations is that a political entrepreneur will make an approach to the disenchanted members of the coalition, offering them a better deal through a package of policies tailored to their special concerns. In the end, that is exactly what happened to Mulroney's grand coalition: his Western pillar was seduced by the Reform Party, while his Quebec pillar defected to the Bloc Québécois.

The Pillars Start to Crumble

Mulroney's victory was greeted with euphoria in the West, but euphoria gradually turned to disappointment as the expected changes were slow in coming. Finance Minister Michael Wilson, formerly a Bay Street investment executive, wanted to tackle the deficit, but Mulroney's famous comment that social programs were a "sacred trust" slowed him down.[17] The government gradually balanced the federal operating budget (money spent on programs), but high interest payments on the large debt inherited from the years of Liberal government meant that the deficit and debt kept growing under the Conservative government.[18] In essence, the government was borrowing money to pay the interest on previously borrowed money.

And interest rates were indeed high. I can remember from those days having a first mortgage on our house at 12 percent, a second mortgage at 14 percent, and an equity-takeout mortgage on our former condominium unit at 21 percent – rates that are inconceivable today. Such high interest rates were a response to inflation, which had reached 11 percent in 1980.[19] By 1984, inflation had come down to a range of 5–6 percent, but debt incurred in earlier years often still carried higher rates of interest. Due to such interest payments, the federal government's annual deficit remained high, though some progress was made in reducing it as a share of gross domestic product.

Privatization of thirty Crown corporations, including giants such as Petro-Canada and Air Canada, did come later, but there was little action on that front in the first couple of years of Mulroney's term in office. The National Energy Program was repealed in stages, but by the time it was completely abolished in 1986, world oil prices had fallen precipitously, leading to cynical comments in the West about how Ottawa wanted the surplus revenues when prices were high but was happy to back out when prices were low. The Mulroney government's incremental approach may have made good economic sense, but it risked causing disappointment in the West, where expectations of a Conservative government were high after two decades of Liberal rule.

The flashpoint for Western discontent came in October 1986, when the federal government awarded the maintenance contract for the CF-18 fighter plane to Canadair in Montreal rather than Bristol Aerospace in Winnipeg, even though Bristol's bid was cheaper and had been judged technically superior by an adjudication panel of civil servants. The official explanation that giving the contract to Canadair was in the "national interest" hardly worked in the West. Saskatoon *Star Phoenix* columnist Les MacPherson captured the Western mood with a satirical op-ed that began: "The federal government today announced it would award the Stanley Cup to Quebec, even though Alberta's Calgary Flames won the competition."[20] Mulroney later wrote that the decision to grant the contract to Canadair was sound but had been poorly communicated, because the government was also planning to give a different contract to Bristol for other work. If the two contracts had been announced at the same time, he thought, Western anger could have been avoided.[21] Maybe so, but if there is a general rule of politics, it is that politicians tend to blame their mistakes on miscommunication rather than on the essence of the action.

Be that as it may, the political damage had been done. As seen through Western eyes, the National Energy Program had been devised by a Liberal prime minister from Quebec to benefit the consumers and taxpayers of Eastern Canada, especially Quebec. Now a Conservative prime minister from Quebec was making a decision about industrial policy calculated to benefit Montreal at the expense of Winnipeg. The conclusion seemed obvious to many in the West: their interests would always be subordinated to those of Quebec. In retrospect, this can be identified as the point where the political alliance between the West and Quebec, so essential to Mulroney's great victory in 1984, really started to crumble.

The CF-18 incident gave Preston Manning the opportunity he had been waiting for. Here we need to look at a little history to understand what happened – not the "cooling of the earth," but going back a few decades. The Reform Party was not born out of nothing; it probably would never have gotten off the ground except for Preston Manning's background in Alberta.

Preston was the son of former Alberta Social Credit leader Ernest Manning, who served as premier from 1943 through 1968. Ernest Manning was the protégé of William Aberhart, a Calgary school principal and fundamentalist preacher who founded the Alberta Social Credit League in the depths of the Depression and swept to power in the provincial election of 1935. The term "Social Credit" was derived from the eccentric theories of British monetary reformer C.H. Douglas. Scorned by conventional economists, the theories of Douglas, as expounded by Aberhart, nonetheless gave hope to Albertans rendered desperate by unemployment, low agricultural prices, and staggering debt loads during the Depression.[22]

To be implemented in Alberta, Social Credit theory would have required the province to opt out of the Canadian financial system and distribute its own means of exchange, ridiculed as "funny money" by its detractors, based on the potential "social credit" of the province rather than on conventional bank reserves. Social Credit policy was unconstitutional because it challenged federal control over money and banking,[23] and it proved impossible to implement in practice, so after Aberhart's death in 1943, Ernest Manning steered the province in a more conventional centre-right direction. The transition was eased by the discovery of oil at Leduc in 1947, which enabled Manning to pay off the province's debts and introduce the best-funded array of public services in Canada.[24] The name Manning became synonymous in Alberta with prosperity, prudent administration, and traditional values, bolstered by Manning's evangelistic role on the "Back to the Bible Hour" radio broadcast.

In the mid-1960s, towards the end of his career in office, Ernest Manning worked on a project to unify the federal Progressive Conservative Party with the federal wing of Social Credit, to build a party that could compete on equal terms with the Liberals. He also contemplated a merger of the Alberta Social Credit League with the provincial Progressive Conservatives, whom he saw headed for a revival under their new leader, the charismatic young lawyer Peter Lougheed. Manning enlisted his son Preston to work in behind-the-scenes negotiations and to help write a book about the proposal.[25] Preston was a rather wonkish young man, well suited to research, writing, and confidential discussions with Lougheed's assistant, Joe Clark.

After the merger failed, Ernest Manning retired from politics at the end of 1968 and founded a consulting firm in partnership with Preston, who developed his father's dream of a merger of existing parties into a vision of a new national party based in the West, modelled on populist forebears such as the United Farmers of Alberta, the Progressives, and Social Credit. For Preston, the CF-18 incident provided the opportunity to found a new party. He had powerful media support in that endeavour from Ted Byfield's *Alberta Report*.[26] Probably few remember it today, but the *Alberta Report* was a stoutly conservative and Western populist provincial news magazine with high circulation in Alberta and to a lesser degree in the other Western provinces. Manning pulled together discontented people from several provincial and federal parties and from all four Western provinces for the Western Assembly on Canada's Economic and Political Future, held in Vancouver at the end of May 1987. That assembly led to foundation of the Reform Association and then the Reform Party of Canada, incorporated in 1988 at a convention in Winnipeg. It was a new party, to be sure, but it also incarnated political ideas that had been percolating in the West, especially Alberta, for decades.

Initially, the Reform Party's main concern was the perceived mistreatment of the West. The demand for a "Triple-E Senate" – equal, elected, and effective – became its great rallying cry. The idea was that an elected Senate, in which each of the four Western provinces would have as many seats as Ontario or Quebec, would be a bulwark against policies like the National Energy Program, which had been supported by voting majorities in Central Canada. In the tradition of populism, Reform also stood for direct democracy – referendum, initiative, and recall – as a supplement to parliamentary government. It advocated balanced budgets, reminding voters that the Mulroney government was not making as much progress on that front as it had promised. Policy details were provided by the young Stephen Harper, born in Ontario but now a graduate student in economics at the University of Calgary and a sessional lecturer at Mount Royal College.[27] Appointed Chief Policy Officer by Manning, Harper put together an entire Blue Book of Western-oriented policies, which remained the party's de facto campaign platform until Reform morphed into the Canadian Alliance in 2000.

In the short run, the damage to the Progressive Conservatives was minimal. Although Reform ran seventy-two candidates in the 1988 election, the party got only 2 percent of the vote and failed to elect anyone. Mulroney's decision to give the CF-18 contract to Montreal-based Canadair rather than Winnipeg-based Bristol Aerospace seemed to have received political validation. But that was in the short run. In 1993, only five years later, Mulroney's electoral prospects had become so poor that he resigned as leader, setting the stage for the repudiation of the Progressive Conservatives under their new leader, Kim Campbell.

Switching focus now to Quebec, Mulroney turned to constitutional reform to cement the support of that pillar. In the 1985 provincial election campaign, won by the Liberals, Premier Robert Bourassa had outlined five conditions for Quebec to approve the constitutional amendments of 1982. These included recognition of Quebec as a "distinct society," a Quebec veto over constitutional change, a provincial role in the appointment of Supreme Court justices from Quebec, greater provincial control over immigration, and limits on the federal spending power.[28]

At a first ministers meeting in Edmonton in 1986, Mulroney got the premiers to agree to a "Quebec Round" of constitutional changes based on Bourassa's five conditions. They reached unanimous agreement at a meeting at Meech Lake (the prime minister's vacation retreat outside Ottawa) on April 30, 1987. The Meech Lake Accord, as it became known, incorporated all of Bourassa's five demands, though the constitutional veto for Quebec was provided by extending the reach of the unanimity rule for approval of amendments. That is, Quebec would have a veto because all provinces would have a veto. Compared to the later Charlottetown Accord, the Meech Lake Accord was a relatively short document almost entirely focused on Bourassa's five conditions, which constituted Quebec's reply to the enactment of the Canadian Charter of Rights and Freedoms against the wishes of the provincial government in 1982.

Meech Lake seemed to be a good start towards Mulroney's goal of pacifying Quebec and solidifying his grand coalition. All ten provincial premiers were on side, as were the national leaders of the Liberals and the NDP, John Turner and Ed Broadbent. But former prime minister Pierre Trudeau soon upset the applecart. In extravagant language, he condemned Mulroney as a "weakling" and the premiers as "snivelers."[29] Yet in spite of signs that opposition would grow, Mulroney and the premiers formally signed the accord in Ottawa on June 2, 1987, after a difficult nineteen-hour meeting.

The Achilles heel of the Meech Lake Accord was that it required approval by a formal vote of all ten provincial legislatures within three years. The designated date for completion was June 22, 1990. That provision proved to be the cause of the accord's failure because in those three years, elections would result in a change of government and of the legislative majority in Newfoundland, Manitoba, and New Brunswick. The newly elected governments and MLAs were less enthusiastic about the accord than their predecessors; indeed, some were openly opposed. For the time being, however, conditions seemed propitious for the upcoming 1988 federal election. Mulroney had seemingly delivered on his promise to Quebec of constitutional changes that would meet the demands of the province.

Another arrow in Mulroney's quiver was the Free Trade Agreement with the United States. Though the details were vague, President Ronald Reagan had announced his openness to free trade with Canada. Encouraged by Alberta's Premier Peter Lougheed, Mulroney changed his mind about free trade with the United States. In line with the position of many past Conservative leaders, he had opposed it in his 1983 leadership campaign,[30] but he entered into negotiations with the United States in 1986. The result was a draft agreement that became the centrepiece of the 1988 election campaign in Canada.

NDP leader Ed Broadbent came out strongly against free trade, so much so that Liberal leader John Turner, fearing the NDP could displace the Liberals as official opposition, also went all out against the agreement, even though free trade with the United States was the historical position of the Liberal Party. Of course, there were other issues in the campaign, but free trade came to dominate everything. In effect, the 1988 election became almost a referendum on free trade with the United States.[31]

From an electoral point of view, that was a good thing for Mulroney and the Conservatives. They were the only party supporting free trade, while the Liberals and the NDP vied with each other over who could oppose it most vocally. At all times, polls showed a majority of Canadians opposed free trade with the United States, but those opposing votes were split between two parties, while the largest single bloc of votes went to Mulroney's Conservatives. Also, free trade was an issue, perhaps the only issue, that could bring the Quebec and Western pillars of Mulroney's grand coalition together. It was devastating to the prospects of the Reform Party in the West. Reform couldn't oppose free trade outright without renouncing its general free market orientation, so Manning criticized it on the grounds that it hadn't been "honestly communicated."[32] As a voter who might have been interested in Reform, I decided to stick with the Conservatives, because I thought it was more important to approve the free trade agreement. Many other Western Conservatives who eventually came over to Reform as I did thought the same way in 1988.

The 1988 election results appeared to vindicate Mulroney's management of the issues. The Conservatives maintained a healthy majority of seats, with 43 percent of the popular vote and 169 of 295 seats. They increased their Quebec results to 53 percent of the provincial vote and 63 seats. They lost some ground in the West, dropping from 58 to 48 seats, but that was still a majority of the 86 seats in the region. Overall, it seemed that the Conservative grand coalition was still standing, albeit slightly battered. Within five years, however, it would fall apart completely as all three pillars – the West, Ontario, and Quebec – came crashing down.

2

Collapse of the Coalition

IN CHAPTER 1, we looked at how Brian Mulroney built the grand coalition that brought the Conservatives to power in 1984 and kept them in office after the 1988 election. We now take a look at how that coalition collapsed.

The cracks in the pillars of Mulroney's grand coalition began showing soon after the 1988 election. In March 1989, Reformer Deborah Grey won a by-election in Beaver River, Alberta. The Progressive Conservative who had won in the general election of 1988 had died shortly thereafter, having concealed from voters that he was suffering from terminal cancer. Grey, a physical education teacher and political neophyte, defeated the previous incumbent's widow for the vacant seat.[1] Then in October of the same year, Reformer Stan Waters, a Second World War hero well known in Alberta business circles, finished first in an Alberta advisory election race to fill a Senate vacancy.[2]

It was the prime minister's constitutional right to recommend senatorial appointments to the Governor General, but he could take advice from the results of an advisory election if he wished. There had already been pressure from Reform to hold the election as part of its drive for a Triple-E Senate. Alberta premier Don Getty was not a Reformer; in fact, he was quite hostile to the new party. Like many other Albertans, however, he supported the idea of an elected Senate and so had legislation passed to enable advisory elections. Mulroney, needing to keep all the premiers on side to get the Meech Lake Accord ratified, decided to appease Getty by appointing Waters to the Senate. Like Getty, Mulroney was no friend of Reform, and he did not favour an elected Senate, but there is always a hierarchy of imperatives in politics, and at the moment getting the Meech Lake Accord ratified was more important to the prime minister than worrying about how one Senate vacancy was to be filled.

Meanwhile, a new problem was arising. Mulroney had decided to carry through with his promise to replace the Manufacturers' Sales Tax (MST) with a new Goods and Services Tax (GST), even though all provincial governments except Quebec's were opposed to his plan to merge the GST with provincial sales taxes. The legislation was introduced in the House of Commons on January 24, 1990.[3] The Conservatives had the votes to pass it in the House, but, as a highly visible tax replacing the hidden MST, it proved unpopular with voters, and the other parties lined up to delay it. The Liberals still had a majority in the Senate as a holdover from many years of Pierre Trudeau's appointments to that body. When the Senate refused to pass the GST legislation transmitted from the House of Commons, Mulroney used section 26 of the Constitution Act, 1867 to ask the Queen to appoint eight additional senators. He then nominated Conservatives to create a majority in the Senate to pass the legislation, which came into effect in January 1991.

Students of public finance generally regard the GST as a big improvement over the MST, but getting it enacted required a bruising political fight that weakened Mulroney's ability to rally support for his constitutional agenda. And the Meech Lake Accord was headed for serious trouble. Elections in New Brunswick, Manitoba, and Newfoundland in the years 1987 through 1989 caused

Manitoba MLA Elijah Harper holds the eagle
feather that would become famous as a symbol
of his vote against the Meech Lake Accord, June
19, 1990. | Wayne Glowacki, *Winnipeg Free Press*

these provinces' governments to change before the accord could be
ratified. The three-year deadline fell on June 22, 1990, and Manitoba
and Newfoundland failed to ratify by that date. In Manitoba, the
accord was effectively blocked by NDP member Elijah Harper,
the only Indigenous member of the Legislative Assembly. A former
chief of the Red Sucker Lake First Nation, Harper had been a
member of the NDP cabinet until the Conservatives won the 1988
provincial election. The new Conservative premier, Gary Filmon,
wanted to support the accord, but he needed unanimous consent
from all members of the legislature to approve the procedure for
voting, and Harper repeatedly denied consent on the grounds that
there had been no Indigenous consultation. The picture of Elijah
Harper holding an eagle feather as he voted no achieved iconic
status across Canada. His successful blocking manoeuvre signalled

that Indigenous people would have to be at the table in future constitutional negotiations.

The Manitoba legislature adjourned on June 22, 1990, without approving the accord. This became the rationale for Clyde Wells, Liberal premier of Newfoundland, to cancel a scheduled ratifica- tion vote in his legislature. Wells had never been enthusiastic about Meech, and now he could say that the accord was dead in any case because it had not been ratified in Manitoba.

The period leading up to the failure of the Meech Lake Accord was tumultuous. The Supreme Court of Canada had decided in the 1988 *Ford* case that Quebec's legislation requiring outdoor signs to be French-only violated the freedom of speech provision in sec- tion 2 of the Canadian Charter of Rights and Freedoms.[4] Immediately after the *Ford* decision, Quebec resorted to use of the notwith- standing clause (section 33 of the Charter) to preserve its language legislation, which gave rise to second thoughts elsewhere. Some people thought that if that was Quebec's attitude, why should the rest of the country go to such efforts to placate the province? Mulroney deputized Jean Charest to chair a commission that would ease the concerns of opponents.

Charest was a young, perfectly bilingual, politically talented, and ambitious lawyer from Sherbrooke, Quebec. First elected in 1984, he was appointed to cabinet in 1986 at the age of twenty-eight, making him the youngest cabinet minister in Canadian history.[5] He temporarily blotted his copybook in 1990 when he called a judge about pending litigation and had to resign from cabinet. But he was always a favourite of Mulroney, who appointed him to blunt the opposition developing against Meech Lake. Charest would return to cabinet the next year and run for Conservative leader in 1993. As the only former cabinet minister re-elected in 1993, he assumed the Conservative leadership after Kim Campbell resigned, and ul- timately became Liberal premier of Quebec (the Liberals were, at that time, the most ideologically conservative party in Quebec provincial politics). If he failed in the Meech Lake assignment, it was not through lack of political ability but because of the intractable dilemmas that the accord now presented.

Charest's recommendation was for a companion accord that would assert the primacy of the Charter over Meech Lake's distinct society clause, and would also assert the responsibility of the federal government to promote minority languages, including English in Quebec.[6] Because this seemed to repudiate his use of the notwithstanding clause, Quebec premier Robert Bourassa rejected the recommendations of the Charest Commission. Even more seriously for Mulroney, his old friend Lucien Bouchard turned against him in May 1990, believing that Quebec, which had been the first to ratify Meech, was now being treated dishonourably by attempts to modify the substance of the accord.

Bouchard and Mulroney had been close friends at Laval law school, even though their politics were different, Bouchard being left-wing and nationalist whereas Mulroney was right-wing and federalist. Their paths crossed again in the 1970s, when both were associated with the investigation of the Cliche Commission into corruption in organized labour in Quebec. Soon after Mulroney became prime minister, he appointed Bouchard ambassador to France, even though Bouchard had supported the yes side in the 1980 Quebec referendum on sovereignty-association. Then he asked Bouchard to come back to Canada to run as a Conservative in 1988 and personally campaigned for him. After Bouchard was elected, Mulroney appointed him secretary of state, an important position at the time for a francophone minister from Quebec because the portfolio included cultural programs. Mulroney later named Bouchard minister of the environment and Quebec lieutenant.[7]

Bouchard had initially been satisfied with the Meech Lake Accord but thought that Jean Charest's recommendation for a companion accord would weaken the distinct society clause beyond the point of acceptability. He saw it as an insult to Quebec to derogate from Bourassa's five conditions at the last minute in order to get acceptance from the other provinces. When he was in Europe, he made a public statement without consulting Mulroney, leading to his resignation from cabinet (his version) or expulsion (Mulroney's version). Deeply wounded, Mulroney regarded Bouchard's actions as a stab in the back. "I have never known a more vulgar expression of betrayal and deceit," he later told journalist Peter Newman.[8]

But the situation was even more dangerous than the rupture of an old friendship. Bouchard quickly moved to found a new political party, the Bloc Québécois, to promote the sovereign independence of Quebec. He brought with him five other members of the Conservative caucus as well as two from the Liberals. He anticipated correctly that the Bloc could win more than fifty seats in Quebec in the next federal election, but he thought incorrectly that this would lead to a minority government in which the Bloc would hold the balance of power and could use its leverage to promote the independence of Quebec.[9] Like most observers at the time, he thought that Reform might win seats in the West but could not foresee that the rise of the party would so badly wound the Progressive Conservatives in Ontario that the Liberals would cruise to a majority government.

In a by-election held in August 1990, the Bloc elected its first new member to the House of Commons, Gilles Duceppe, a union organizer and former Maoist. The recruitment of Duceppe illustrated Bouchard's conception of a trans-ideological party mustering support from all points on the political spectrum in order to promote the independence of Quebec. It was in some ways similar to Preston Manning's original conception of Reform as neither left, centre, nor right but dedicated to promoting the interests of the West. Whatever the precise colour of this political chameleon, it was a threat to the Conservatives because the Bloc appealed directly to their francophone supporters in Quebec.

Only six years after the sweeping victory of 1984, Mulroney's grand coalition was now in mortal peril as two of its three pillars were threatened with collapse. In the West, long-time Conservative supporters seemed as if they might defect to Preston Manning and Reform, while Quebec Conservatives, whose roots in the party were much shallower, were attracted to the Bloc and Lucien Bouchard. Without Quebec and the West, the Conservatives would no longer be a party of government, maybe not even a party at all. This was the gravest threat to a national party since the Progressives stole most of the Western Liberal support in the election of 1921. Liberal prime minister Mackenzie King handled that challenge subtly and successfully; what would Mulroney do? He had to do something, for Premier Bourassa had announced that there would be another Quebec referendum in 1992, either on sovereignty or on a new proposal from Canada. Meanwhile, said Bourassa, the government of Quebec would not engage in constitutional discussions as one of ten provinces; it would hold its own discussions preparatory to receiving a new offer from Canada.

Rescue Attempt: The Charlottetown Accord

Mulroney's response was to pursue constitutional change on an even grander scale, attempting to deal with at least some of the criticisms that had dogged the Meech Lake process. One was that Meech was entirely focused on the concerns of Quebec, leaving out the rest of the country. In one sense, this was obviously true: from the beginning, Meech had been the "Quebec round," supposedly to be followed by later discussions of other topics. But critics of Meech feared that granting Quebec a constitutional veto by extension of the unanimity formula meant that future talks on subjects such as Senate reform could never get off the ground.

Another criticism was that the Meech process had been too closed. Everything was negotiated by "men in suits," first ministers meeting behind closed doors. Again, this was obviously true: the

Meech process had followed the traditional protocols of executive federalism featuring confidential negotiations, although there was also a more democratic stage at the end because of the need for ratification of constitutional amendments in elected legislatures. Related to both of these was opposition by Indigenous leaders trying to claim a role for themselves in ratifying constitutional amendments. Elijah Harper's actions in the Manitoba legislature had triggered the failure of the Meech Lake Accord in 1990, so it was obvious there would have to be some level of Indigenous support for a new accord if it was to have any hope of passing.

To meet the criticisms, Mulroney did what Trudeau had done before him to get the Canadian Charter of Rights and Freedoms approved – he expanded the agenda of constitutional change. In the beginning, Trudeau had been focused on Quebec, thinking that entrenchment of official bilingualism and a charter of rights in the constitution would hold off the nascent movement of Quebec separatism. In his famous speech in May 1980, just before Quebec's first referendum on sovereignty-association, Trudeau said: "I know that I can make a most solemn commitment that following a NO vote, we will immediately take action to renew the Constitution and we will not stop until we have done that."[10] But his idea of constitutional change remained what it always had been – protection for official bilingualism in Canada as part of a charter of rights. Now, to get the support of the provinces, he sought the endorsement of what became known as "Charter groups" – women, Aboriginals, and multicultural minorities. Ironically, he ended up getting the English provinces on side while losing Quebec; but with his huge majority of MPs from Quebec, he felt secure enough to "patriate the constitution" – thereby adding a new verb, "to patriate," to the English language, at least as spoken in Canada.

Mulroney now embarked on a somewhat similar course of action, and, like everything about the man, it was on a grand scale. In spring 1991, he named his old rival Joe Clark as minister responsible for constitutional affairs, with a mandate to prepare a new package of constitutional amendments that might be acceptable to Quebec, the other provinces, and the many special interest groups that had now become stakeholders in the process of constitutional change. After losing the Progressive Conservative leadership to Mulroney in 1983, Clark had remained in politics and had run again as a Conservative candidate in 1984. Mulroney named him minister of foreign affairs, in which post observers thought he acquitted himself well. Clark's long experience in Canadian politics, his prestige as a former prime minister (if only briefly), and his more recent role in international negotiations looked like good preparation for trying to bring together Canada's fractious provinces, as well as interest and opinion groups, around a constitutional reform proposal.

Mulroney also appointed a special parliamentary committee to solicit reactions to a government draft titled *Shaping Canada's Future Together*, plus a Citizens' Forum on Canada's Future, chaired by former commissioner of official languages Keith Spicer, to hold public sessions and in other ways gather public opinion. The "Canada Round" was well and truly underway.

There followed a year of seemingly non-stop meetings, public forums, and news releases about constitutional change. Four national Aboriginal organizations became major players, meeting on a regular basis with ministers and officials of Canada, the provinces, and the territories. Even though these meetings and discussions dominated the headlines for a year, we need not pursue them in detail, except to say that they led to the Consensus Report, popularly known as the Charlottetown Accord, approved on August 28, 1992, at a first ministers meeting in Prince Edward Island. The choice of Charlottetown for the final meeting was deliberate and symbolic, for that is where discussions on what became the British North America Act first took place in 1864. The symbolic message was that the Charlottetown Accord of 1992 would be Canada's new constitution, or at least a sweeping modernization.

It was indeed a sweeping set of proposals, touching all of Canada's major political institutions – the House of Commons, the Senate, the Supreme Court, and federalism. There would be a sort of Triple-E Senate, a guaranteed proportion of seats for Quebec in the House of Commons, elaborate procedures for breaking deadlocks between the House and the Senate, repeal of the federal powers of reservation and disallowance, and much, much more.

In spite of being styled a consensus document, the Charlottetown Accord suffered from a severe weakness that led to its downfall in the subsequent referendum. Very few of the sixty sections contained legal language that could be enacted as constitutional amendments. They were mostly statements of intent, often explicitly coupled with the need for further negotiations. It was difficult to say exactly what the Charlottetown Accord would mean in practice. It seemed in many ways like an agenda for future constitutional negotiations rather than a set of constitutional amendments.

After some initial hesitation on Preston Manning's part, the Reform Party moved to exploit this weakness. Manning's chief policy officer, Stephen Harper, produced an annotated copy of the accord showing how almost every section required further discussions, and the party distributed it widely. Manning had a genius for slogans, and he came up with a good one for Reform's campaign against the accord: "Know More."[11] If you said it aloud with the right intonation, it sounded like "No More," meaning no more giving in to demands from Quebec. When you read it on the printed page, it suggested that you couldn't support the accord because the whole story wasn't being told. It was a perfect slogan for populist voters suspicious of elite deal making. Raising suspicions is a standard technique for defeating complex referendum proposals in jurisdictions, such as California, where frequent referendums are held. As one American author has written: "The initial strategy is to raise doubts about the need, implementation, or impact of the measure. This may result in persons shifting from 'yes' to 'no,' or it may mean that voters shift from support to indecision and then later respond to the appeal – 'when in doubt VOTE NO.'"[12]

Quebec's original concerns, summarized in Premier Bourassa's five conditions, could be found addressed more or less in the Charlottetown Accord if one looked carefully, but it was by no means a Quebec-centred document. Far more space was devoted to topics such as Senate reform and an Aboriginal "third order of government," which Quebec had never asked for. Quebec's reasonably well-focused original demands had morphed into a sprawling set of constitutional changes, many of which were irrelevant to Quebec, perhaps even hostile to the constitutional interests of the province's political class. It was a classic case of mission creep, in which the original purpose had almost disappeared.

Most fundamentally, the strategy of trying to give something to everyone – Senate reform for the West, self-government for Aboriginals, an economic charter for social democrats, nods towards feminist and multicultural advocates, and on and on – had produced a document that no one had ever asked for or really wanted. Many politically active groups might find something that they liked in the accord, but for most people it contained far more that they couldn't understand or actively disliked. In contrast, the Meech Lake Accord, despite its failure to be ratified, had reflected the demands of Quebec provincial politicians and had their support. But literally no one had asked for the assemblage of changes in the Charlottetown Accord. Those who supported it did so not because they liked the whole thing but because they wanted the process to end and thought they could live with the Charlottetown Accord if they had to. Joe Clark later summarized the situation elegantly: "We had needed a large package to get any agreement at all, but once the campaign began to slide, the size of the package hastened its fall."[13]

Richard Johnston, an eminent political scientist at the University of British Columbia who co-authored the definitive book on the 1992 referendum, called it an "inverted logroll."[14] In political science, the term "logroll" refers to the kind of vote trading that often takes place in the United States Congress: "You support my bill and I'll support yours." Everybody gets something they want. But in describing the Charlottetown Accord as an inverted logroll, Johnston emphasized that all participants were getting a lot of things that they didn't want   there was so much unwanted stuff that it outweighed the one or two things that they actually did want.

The legal process for ratification of the Charlottetown Accord was the same as for Meech – an affirmative vote in Parliament and ratification in the legislatures of all ten provinces. There was a new complication, however: Quebec, Alberta, and British Columbia had enacted legislation requiring that a popular referendum be held in the province before the legislative vote. Legally, such referendums would be only consultative, but in practice it was unlikely that any legislature would ignore the results of a referendum within its own borders. Realizing that it was untenable for some provinces to hold referendums while others did not, the federal government had Parliament pass a federal constitutional referendum act.[15] In the event, Quebec would hold its referendum under its own rules, while the other nine provinces would vote under the federal procedure.

Because the referendum was legally advisory rather than binding, it was never quite clear how the results should be interpreted. What if there was an overall yes vote but one or more provinces voted no? Should the legislatures of those provinces withhold approval because there were more no voters than yes voters in their province? These were interesting questions, but they didn't matter in the end because the referendum result was clearly negative.

As the referendum campaign got underway on September 11, 1992, polls were reporting that well over 50 percent of decided voters intended to vote yes, making it look like a walkover for the yes side.[16] This wasn't surprising, given that the Charlottetown Accord was supported by the governments of Canada and all the provinces; by the old-line political parties – Conservatives, Liberals, and NDP –

both federally and provincially; by the corporate media, both print and broadcast; by big business and organized labour; and by a wide variety of other organizations. Indeed, it seemed that everybody who was anybody would support the accord – except, as it turned out, a majority of the voters.

In the event, the referendum delivered one of the most surprising results in Canadian history, with voters declining to follow the most prominent political and civic leaders. In retrospect, it looks like an early harbinger of contemporary populist rebellions in countries such as the United States and the United Kingdom, where large numbers of voters supported Donald Trump and the Brexit movement, respectively, against the advice of better-known and more established leaders.

Support for the yes side started to slip almost immediately. Even though the federal Liberal Party and its leader, Jean Chrétien, supported the accord, Pierre Trudeau attacked it in *Maclean's* magazine and in a speech delivered at the Maison Egg Roll restaurant in Montreal on October 1. The speech was quickly printed in English under the title "A Mess that Deserves a Big NO," which needs little further elaboration.[17] The opposition of Reform leader Preston Manning was also important, because he and Trudeau appealed to different audiences for different reasons. Trudeau, speaking to Liberals, evoked fears that the Charlottetown Accord would lead to the oppression of linguistic minorities who were supposed to be protected by the Charter. Manning, heard mainly by Western voters, particularly those who had previously supported Brian Mulroney and the Progressive Conservatives, evoked fears of favouritism towards Quebec. NDP leaders supported the accord, but when the votes were counted, results showed that the party could not deliver its working-class supporters.

All three old-line parties were deeply divided over the accord, even though their official leadership supported it. Similar splits occurred in Quebec. The Quebec Liberals campaigned on the yes side, but prominent provincial Liberals such as Jean Allaire and Mario Dumont joined the no campaign. The Charlottetown Accord was a battering ram that smashed old political alignments, especially Mulroney's grand coalition, even as the supporters of new parties – Reform, the Bloc Québécois, and the Parti Québécois – were united against it.

Of course, opponents of the accord rejected it for contradictory reasons. Those who followed Trudeau saw it as a threat to the rights of linguistic and ethnic minorities, fearing that Charter guarantees could be overridden in Quebec by invoking the distinct society clause. Reformers thought it gave too much to Quebec and not enough to the West, that its version of Senate reform was inadequate, that it would do nothing to stop runaway deficit spending. Quebec nationalists led by Lucien Bouchard and Jacques Parizeau argued that it was another insult to Quebec because it watered down the new jurisdictions and guarantees they thought they had achieved in the Meech Lake Accord. But there is no rule in democracy that opposition has to be coherent. Voters may have many different and contradictory reasons for thinking that a proposed innovation is worse than the status quo.[18]

On the yes side, there was little detailed defence of the accord outside Quebec. Proponents told voters it was the best deal to be had, so they should vote yes to end the years of constitutional wrangling.[19] They even tried to frighten voters by telling them that the separation of Quebec and thus the breakup of Canada were inevitable unless the accord was approved – but not enough voters were intimidated.

In Quebec, Mulroney tried to emphasize what the province would gain from the accord. In a speech at Sherbrooke, he dramatically tore up a list of these supposed gains "and threw it on the floor in front of a startled audience."[20] The humour magazine *Frank* memorably skewered Mulroney's gesture as "pieces in our time," alluding to British prime minister Neville Chamberlain's famous

Prime Minister Brian Mulroney tore up a piece of paper representing the Charlottetown Accord to show that a no vote would end Quebec's gains in the Charlottetown Accord, September 28, 1992. | Fred Chartrand, *The Canadian Press*

1938 statement that he had achieved "peace for our time" by agreeing to Hitler's dismemberment of Czechoslovakia.

But the voters were not intimidated, neither in Quebec nor in the rest of Canada. Almost thirty years after the referendum, Quebec is still part of Canada and separatism is much less powerful than it once was, so perhaps the voters were wiser than the elites – although, to be fair, the separatist side came very close to winning a sovereignty referendum in Quebec in 1995. If the 1995 vote had been only a few tenths of a percentage point different, Quebec might have separated, and we might today be lamenting the failure of voters to follow their leaders. We can never know the future, and politics is always a gamble.

The results of the vote held on October 26, 1992, are shown in Table 2.1, with the provinces listed from west to east. Only the provincial results are shown because, although the referendum was

TABLE 2.1
Results of the 1992 referendum on the Charlottetown Accord (%)

Jurisdiction	Yes	No	Turnout
British Columbia	31.7	60.2	72.6
Alberta	39.8	60.2	76.7
Saskatchewan	44.7	55.3	68.7
Manitoba	38.4	61.6	70.6
Ontario	50.1	49.9	71.9
Quebec	43.3	56.7	82.8
New Brunswick	61.8	31.2	72.2
Nova Scotia	48.8	51.2	67.8
Prince Edward Island	73.9	26.2	70.5
Newfoundland	63.2	36.8	53.3

Source: Electronic Frontier Canada, "Charlottetown Accord Referendum Results,"
September 26, 1994, http://www.efc.ca/pages/law/cons/Constitutions/Canada/English/
Proposals/charlottetown-res.html.

also held in the territories, the territorial legislatures did not have a right to vote on the accord. As creatures of federal legislation, they were included in Parliament's vote.

The no side prevailed overall, 54.3 percent against 45.7 percent, winning majorities in six out of ten provinces. It was clear repudiation of the Charlottetown Accord, eliminating the possibility that it could still be ratified after some tweaking. It was dead.

Since 1992, there have been no serious attempts to resuscitate the accord or implement other so-called mega-constitutional change. Smaller-scale amendments of some importance have been passed, such as changes to the school systems in Quebec and Newfoundland, but no one has been brave or foolhardy enough to essay another major rewrite of the Constitution. The passions unleashed by Trudeau's successful amendments in 1982 and Mulroney's failed attempts in 1987 and 1992 have burned themselves out, and Canadians seem willing to live with their Constitution, with only a nip and a tuck from time to time.

In addition to demonstrating the general difficulty of mega-constitutional change, the referendum also previewed voting patterns that would become obvious in the election of 1993 and beyond. All four Western provinces rejected the Charlottetown Accord, and the Reform Party went on to win a majority of Western seats in the House of Commons in 1993. Quebec also rejected the accord in the referendum, and the new Bloc Québécois went on to win a majority of seats in that province in 1993. The 1992 referendum vote was obviously a good, though not perfect, predictor of how provinces would vote in the 1993 election. A no vote meant receptivity to one of the new parties, with the only exception being Nova Scotia, which voted no in 1992 but stuck with the Liberals in 1993.

Other important trends were also present beneath the surface. The no vote, which dominated the four Western provinces, was much stronger in rural areas than in cities. Indeed, as was often remarked, Preston Manning's own high-income urban riding, Calgary Southwest, voted yes. In 1993, the rural West would trend towards Reform, while the Liberals and NDP would hold on to some urban seats in the region. The urban-rural divide was also important in Ontario, which voted yes narrowly overall but by a large majority in the major cities of Toronto and Ottawa. Similarly, Reform would do much better in the 1993 election in rural Ontario than in the major cities. And in Quebec, large majorities for the no side in the francophone ridings turned into victories for the Bloc Québécois in the same ridings in 1993.

With the all-important benefit of hindsight, the 1992 referendum was clearly a harbinger of the 1993 election. Yet things were not quite so clear at the time. Voters at first seemed to make a distinction between voting in a referendum and voting in an election. Reform support had peaked at 16 percent early in 1992, but gradually drifted downward to a low of 6 percent at the end of that year; Manning's personal ratings (balance of negative over positive) also declined throughout 1992.[21] Reform's slippage may have been caused at least in part by Manning's initial wavering over the Charlottetown Accord followed by his all-out assault on the "Mulroney Deal," as he called it, echoing the language the Liberals had used against the Free Trade Agreement in the 1988 election. The idealism of the new party seemed eclipsed by the grubby realities of campaign tactics. Or perhaps it was just that Reform's popularity in 1992 was linked to the unpopularity of the Charlottetown Accord. For some voters, once the accord had been defeated, Reform as a new party without an established brand was no longer top of mind when it came to answering pollsters' questions.

Kim Campbell Steps to the Fore

Whatever the precise reason for Reform's temporary decline, it gave the battered Conservatives hope that they could bounce back under new leadership. Realizing that he had become the most unpopular party leader since the rise of public opinion polling, Mulroney announced on February 24, 1993, that he would resign as prime minister, to be replaced by a new Conservative leader in June after the necessary leadership race.

There were five candidates for the Conservative leadership but only two major ones – Minister of Justice Kim Campbell and Minister of the Environment Jean Charest. Importantly, Campbell came from the West (British Columbia) and Charest came from Quebec – the two pillars of Mulroney's grand coalition that had been so profoundly shaken by the long struggles over the Meech Lake and Charlottetown Accords. It is striking, however, that none of the real heavyweights in Mulroney's cabinet, people like Michael Wilson and Joe Clark, chose to seek the leadership. Campbell and Charest were both relatively recent arrivals on the federal political scene and would have been considered junior figures if Mulroney had not deliberately boosted their cabinet careers.

Jean Charest was introduced earlier in this chapter; now let's say something about Kim Campbell. She was born and grew up in British Columbia. She pursued but did not finish a PhD program in Soviet government, then obtained a law degree from the University of British Columbia. She practised law briefly, but her real love was politics. She was elected to the Vancouver School Board and then the provincial legislature as a member of the Social Credit Party before winning a seat in the House of Commons as a Conservative in the 1988 federal election. Mulroney thought she showed promise and appointed her to several cabinet positions, including the senior portfolios of Justice and National Defence. Because of Mulroney's support, she was able to accumulate an unusual amount of executive experience for a first-term MP.

From the beginning of the leadership race, Campbell was considered the front-runner. Her slogan of "doing politics differently" was meant to emphasize that she would not govern like Mulroney, though the differences were not easy to communicate because she was still in Mulroney's cabinet. Mulroney, in fact, was quite insistent that leadership contenders remain in cabinet while the race took place. Campbell later recalled:

> Brian Mulroney angry is not a comforting sight. I had rarely seen him in such a rage as he displayed in P & P [Policy and Priorities Committee, basically the "inner cabinet"] on March 9 over the idea that a minister might resign in order to become a leadership candidate. He didn't name names, but my cheeks burned because I knew he must have known I'd been discussing stepping down with a number of people. I was absolutely stunned when he insisted furiously that he would regard such a move as a sign of disloyalty.[22]

Having to remain in cabinet was an important hindrance for both Campbell and Charest. As cabinet ministers, they would be bound by the convention of cabinet solidarity and would find it more difficult to articulate how their government would differ from the now unpopular Mulroney government. Yet the fact that Campbell was female did help to distance her from Mulroney. A famous photograph of her standing bare-shouldered and holding her Queen's Counsel robes in front of her helped reinforce the point [23]

Campbell's leadership campaign, even though victorious, showed some weaknesses, however. She demonstrated a certain maladroitness that would haunt her in the 1993 general election. For instance, she told a gathering of street people in Vancouver, "I know that a lot of you have faced disappointment in your lives. I have, too. I wanted more than anything to be a concert cellist."[24] Her orchestral remarks probably did not make them feel better about sleeping on the streets!

Campbell didn't like the draft speeches her team was giving her, but they seemed unable to give her what she wanted. "Speech notes arrived nerve-rackingly late," she later wrote.[25] Ordinarily, aides who can't get necessary materials to the leader in time don't last long in their jobs. Most leaders will fire or reassign such people until they get what they want, but she did not.

She presented herself as different from Mulroney but did not demonstrate the difference with new policy proposals. How could she, since she was still in Mulroney's cabinet? So it had to be all about process and personality. In the end, Campbell defeated Charest, but not by a huge margin – 53 percent to 47 percent on the second ballot at the leadership convention. Some observers used Aesop's fable of the hare and the tortoise to characterize the contest, Campbell being the overconfident hare who jumps out in front but fritters away her lead and Charest being the plodding tortoise who eventually catches up – except that in this case the hare held on to win.[26]

Reading Campbell's description of the leadership race in her autobiography leaves one with the impression that she was not wholly in control of her own campaign. Strikingly, she titled her autobiography *Time and Chance,* based on the Old Testament book of Ecclesiastes (9: 11):

> I returned, and saw under the sun, that the race is not to the swift, nor the battle to the strong, neither yet bread to the wise, nor yet riches to men of understanding, nor yet favour to men of skill; but time and chance happeneth to them all.[27]

The quotation may be good theology, but it is not practical philosophy for a party leader, because it makes her seem passive, a victim of forces outside her control. The message implicit in the title she chose for her autobiography, I think, was that the timing was bad – she inherited the leadership from Mulroney when Conservative fortunes were at a low ebb – and that she was often let down by other people. This may have been true, but successful political leaders cannot be held captive by events but must rise above them, to shape them to their own ends. The air of passivity that runs through her autobiography would surface again in the 1993 election and contribute mightily to the Progressive Conservatives' electoral disaster.

With the advantage of hindsight, it is easy to point out Campbell's political weaknesses that contributed to her lack of success in the 1993 election. Yet any fair assessment must also acknowledge how great her achievement was. In winning the Conservative leadership, she became only the second female leader of a major political party in Canada, Audrey McLaughlin of the NDP having been the first. She also became the first woman to serve as Canadian prime minister, an accomplishment that writers on Canadian politics will forever note. Moreover, no one handed her the big prize; she had to win it in a tough fight against Jean Charest, who was a gifted campaigner. She earned her place in history.

After winning the Conservative leadership and being sworn in as prime minister, Campbell made Jean Charest deputy prime

Prime Minister Kim Campbell waves to the applause of a small group of supporters after her party was defeated, October 25, 1993. Campbell was defeated in her own riding of Vancouver Centre. | Chuck Stoody, The Canadian Press

minister, but this obvious step required considerable arm-twisting by Mulroney,[28] suggesting that her political instincts were not fully matured. Yet that was in private; in public, the Conservatives appeared reunited and revivified. By the end of summer 1993, her personal approval rating was over 50 percent, and the Conservatives and Liberals were both polling in the mid-30s. An internal poll in late August by Alan Gregg's Decima firm showed the Conservatives leading the Liberals 35 percent to 29 percent among decided voters.[29] No one was predicting that Campbell would restore all of Mulroney's grand coalition, but it seemed possible that she could, against all odds, lead her party to another victory – perhaps a narrow one, but still a victory.

Of course, we know that didn't happen. Instead of returning to power, the Conservatives were virtually wiped out. Linda Trimble argues that

> Campbell's campaign was doomed to failure. Her predecessor's popularity had dipped into the single digits before his resignation, and the party's approval rating was at a dismal 18 percent before the leadership contest. Afterwards, there was precious little time for Campbell to win the hearts of an electorate hardened against her party.[30]

Yet it is only in hindsight that the fall of the Conservatives seemed inevitable. Popular reaction to Campbell's accession to power suggests that voters were prepared to consider giving the Conservatives another chance under their new leader. At the time, anything seemed possible.

3

The Contestants

IN ONE SENSE, all elections are similar contests of persuasion, in which the participants attempt to build coalitions of support in order to win more seats than their opponents. Over 2,000 years ago, Aristotle identified the three main aspects of persuasion, which he called ethos, pathos, and logos.[1] Ethos is the character of the candidate or party; today we might speak of credibility, image, or brand. Pathos is emotion or passion; nothing much has changed there. And logos is reason, the realm of campaign promises, of which each party has its own list. Voters reach their decisions by triangulating among ethos, pathos, and logos. There is no right or wrong way to do this; voters supply their own weightings to these principles to arrive at their own decisions.

There are two aspects to persuasion. One is choice or preference. Parties and candidates invest time, energy, and money to convince voters *how* to vote. The other aspect is what political scientists usually call mobilization. Voters have to be convinced not just how to vote but also *whether* to vote. Candidates are not elected by preferences registered in opinion polls but by the votes of people who actually take the trouble to cast a ballot. And there is some cost to voting, not just the time and effort to go to the polling place, but also the much larger amount of time and effort required to learn something about the candidates and what they stand for.

Mobilization depends on enthusiasm, either for or against a party or candidate; that is why pathos – emotion – is so important in campaigning. Also, a few extra percentage points of popular vote can be squeezed out by deliberate organization – identifying supporters and contacting them at the right time to "get out the vote" (GOTV).[2]

But even if the essence of elections remains the same, the means of persuasion and mobilization change as time passes. The biggest change since 1993 has been the explosion of digital information technology. In 1993, the Internet was not yet widely used, and social media did not exist. The fax machine was still considered high-tech. Political platforms and pamphlets had to be printed on paper, which put a high premium on dropping off literature at the doorstep. Absence of the Internet also meant that opposition research was more difficult. Compared with more recent elections, fewer candidates were forced to resign during the 1993 campaign because of some sketchy episode dredged up from the past. Without social media, candidates or leaders couldn't post announcements on Facebook or Twitter; they had to issue a press release, hold a news conference, or grant an interview to a reporter. Advertising budgets were spent on television, radio, and newspapers because digital platforms did not exist.

To be sure, some new technology was coming in by 1993. Mobile phones (not smartphones) were now available, though cellular coverage in a country as large as Canada was spotty. Computer databases were also available but were used mainly for fundraising, in conjunction with direct mail and volunteer phone banks. Widespread voter identification and GOTV exercises based on electronic databases were not yet highly developed in Canada, so householders did not have to put up with endless annoying phone calls asking how they intended to vote. Voter identification and GOTV did not become major factors in Canadian elections until after 2004, when the Conservatives began using them on a large scale and the other parties were forced to follow suit.

One innovation in 1993 was the presence of formal written platforms, which had fallen out of favour in the television era of the 1960s and 1970s.[3] As the saying goes, everything old is new again. Preston Manning, who had some old-fashioned ideas about politics, had Stephen Harper draft a platform for the 1988 election and update it for the 1993 campaign, with more input from members' resolutions approved at annual conventions. It became known as the Blue Book, from nineteenth-century terminology for government sessional papers. The Blue Book was actually a policy manual, but it did double duty as a campaign platform. Then Jean Chrétien and the Liberals got into the act with their Red Book, which scholars now see as the prototype of the modern Canadian platform. The Red Book supplied cost estimates for new programs, an innovation that has been widely imitated by other parties. Written platforms are standard again, although they are now posted on the Internet rather than printed, and they are often released in stages to get more leverage in the twenty-four-hour news cycle.

Apart from the absence of the Internet and social media, a campaign conducted in 1993 looked much like one held today. Attention was focused on party leaders, who travelled around the country in the "leader's tour." Leaders and candidates spoke at rallies and held press conferences. Parties made promises about policy and post-election action. They purchased as much advertising as they could afford, chiefly on television. Candidates put up signs in their neighbourhoods and knocked on doors. A contemporary Canadian who time-travelled back to 1993 would not have any trouble understanding what was going on. It would seem a little slow-paced in the absence of the Internet and social media, but otherwise familiar.

Above all, one thing hasn't changed – the first-past-the-post (FPTP) electoral system. In spite of Justin Trudeau's promise in the 2015 election campaign that this would be the last election conducted under FPTP rules, it is still with us.[4] This is extremely important, because the unprecedented outcome of the 1993 election was determined by FPTP, or, more precisely, by the way FPTP interacted with the novel array of parties contending for office. We will examine this in more detail at the end of the next chapter.

The Contestants

Intellectuals often condemn the media for placing too much emphasis on the horse-race aspect of campaigns at the expense of policy. But let's face it: an election is a contest for which a horse race is not a bad analogy. First prize is not a blue ribbon but control of the government. Policies are props that political actors brandish in their dramatic performances seeking the applause of voters. No one can know if the winning party will enact the policies it campaigned on. Perhaps the party's leader wasn't sincere, perhaps conditions have changed, or perhaps the policy sounded good but was too unrealistic for implementation. But one thing is certain: the winners' control of government will give them an opportunity to reward their supporters at the expense of their opponents, even if what they do is not exactly what they campaigned on. In the real world of politics, winning counts for its own sake, just as in a horse race.

So let's handicap the contestants in the 1993 election. We can't assign odds, as real handicappers do, but we can see where the party stood when the writ was dropped and what its prospects appeared to be. The order is roughly from worst to best, not in terms of how well the party actually did in the election but rather in terms of what its prospects appeared to be before the election was called.

Before discussing the major contestants, let's take a quick look at the fringe players. In every election, there are some minor parties that have little or no chance of electing anyone, and 1993 was no exception, with nine smaller parties competing in addition to the main five. It is worth keeping an eye on minor parties because they sometimes develop over time into major contenders. Reform, for example, could have been considered a fringe party in 1988 but had grown into a major force by 1993. The Greens, who barely made a ripple in 1993, were able to run a full nationwide slate of candidates in 2004 and to elect at least one member to the House of Commons in each election from 2011 through 2021.

In 1993, one minor party looked as if it might break out of the pack – the National Party, founded in 1992 by Edmonton bookseller and *Canadian Encyclopedia* publisher Mel Hurtig. The fact that another new party would emerge in Alberta at about the same time as Reform is testimony to the non-conformist tradition of politics in the province. From very early on, Albertans have not been entirely comfortable with the parliamentary system imported from Eastern Canada, and have at various times backed a long series of maverick parties, both federal and provincial. United Farmers of Alberta, Progressives, Social Credit, Reform, and Wildrose are only the best-known names; an even greater number of small parties, like National, never achieved the same level of success.

Mel Hurtig had been a passionate opponent of the Free Trade Agreement with the United States, the central issue of the 1988 election.[5] Together with prominent figures such as Margaret Atwood and David Suzuki, he had founded the Council of Canadians in 1985 to oppose free trade.[6] In 1991, when the Liberals came out in favour of the North American Free Trade Agreement, which would make Mexico a partner to Canada and the United States in the treaty, Hurtig decided he needed his own party. He was able to found such a party because Winnipeg businessman Bill Loewen, also an opponent of free trade, gave $4 million to the cause, perhaps the largest single donation in Canadian political history.[7] The National Party attracted 171 candidates to run in 1993, but it had no real raison d'être. Ideologically, Hurtig and Loewen were trying to squeeze in between the Liberals and the New Democratic Party. The NDP remained opposed to free trade, but, as businessmen, Hurtig and

Loewen didn't like the NDP's close ties with labour unions. The two men were natural supporters of the Liberal Party but couldn't forgive the Liberals for switching to support of free trade. Sadly for the National Party, the NDP and Liberals already overlapped to a considerable degree, and there was very little ideological space for another party in that part of the political spectrum.

Moreover, the National Party lacked geographical concentration. It had a few supporters almost everywhere but not enough supporters anywhere to come close to electing any MPs. Thus someone looking at the National Party before the election would have predicted they would not elect anyone, and that's exactly what happened. In spite of having Loewen's $4 million to spend – a huge amount of money for a new, small party – the National Party was not a real factor in the 1993 election.

Reform Party of Canada

Things didn't look particularly bright for Reform when the election was called. Its popularity had slipped after the exhilaration of the anti-Charlottetown campaign, and it was polling at about 10 percent at the start of the 1993 election campaign.[8] This figure is a bit misleading because Reform was not running candidates in Quebec, so it did not appear as an option in Quebec polling. It would be more accurate to say that Reform was polling at about 12–13 percent in the rest of Canada, where it was contesting the election. Moreover, it was much stronger than that in the West, where it had a real chance of winning some seats.

The party's leadership was an asset in Alberta and British Columbia, where people still remembered Ernest Manning, Preston's father, who had been premier of Alberta from 1943 to 1968. Preston had acquired valuable political experience by founding the Reform Party in 1987 and leading it in the 1988 election, even if the party was only a bit player then. However, the senior ranks of the campaign team were largely inexperienced in national politics, except for campaign manager Rick Anderson, who had worked for the Liberals, albeit not at the highest level.

Money was also an issue. Reform could pay its bills through grassroots fundraising but was largely cut off from the "big money" of corporate and union donations, which at the time still dominated Canadian politics. It also had philosophical objections against going into debt to finance its campaign. Thus, it would not be able to afford the full-scale campaigns of the Liberals and Conservatives, with their national leaders' tours and multimillion-dollar budgets for TV advertising (perhaps a good thing in view of how a late-campaign TV ad would boomerang on the Conservatives in 1993, as will be seen in the next chapter).

The party didn't have a campaign platform as such, but the Blue Book and the Zero in Three plan provided an equivalent. The Blue Book contained all the party's policies approved by delegates at its conventions.[9] Most parties don't trade heavily on such lists because they often contain items that the leader is uncomfortable with. Reform, however, had always printed the Blue Book in large quantities and used it as a recruiting tool.

Zero in Three was a plan for balancing the federal budget in three years after forming a government. It was put together for Manning's approval in the fall of 1992 by Stephen Harper, then Reform's chief policy officer; Harper's assistant, Dimitri Pantazopoulos, now a well-known pollster; and me. It had to be a back-of-the-envelope exercise because we couldn't call upon the Department of Finance and had no money to hire an economic consulting firm. It may have been unrealistic in many details, but overall it was on target, as shown by how the Liberal government did actually eliminate the deficit in three years after being spooked by a possible run on the dollar in 1994.[10]

Zero in Three may not have been perfect, but in the valley of the blind the one-eyed man is king. The Bloc Québécois (BQ) didn't compete with Reform, the NDP didn't appear worried about the deficit, and the Liberals were ambivalent, while the Progressive Conservatives claimed to care but had little credibility after nine years in office during which they had failed to put a stop to deficit spending. Manning could point to Zero in Three and say that, unlike the other leaders, he had an actual plan to balance the budget. It even drew an endorsement from the *Globe and Mail*.[11] Not all voters were concerned with the deficit, but those who gave it high priority were drawn to Reform.

I can remember thinking that Reform would do well to win about a dozen seats in the West, mostly in Alberta, maybe enough to gain the benefits of being an official party in the House of Commons. Preston Manning, in contrast, thought it would win about fifty seats, and he turned out to be right on the money. Real-life political leaders need to be optimists, and their optimism helps them attract supporters. That Reform greatly exceeded the expectations of most observers was due largely to the way the campaign unfolded, as described in the next chapter.

New Democratic Party

The NDP had been on a roller coaster ride since the mid-1980s. With the Liberals floundering under the uncertain leadership of John Turner, it looked as if the NDP might displace them as the official opposition and the main party of the centre-left. Under Ed Broadbent's leadership in the 1988 election, the party had its best performance up to that point, winning 20.4 percent of the national vote and forty-three seats. But politics has never been marked by gratitude. NDP members were disappointed because they had hoped to finish ahead of the Liberals, yet that didn't happen. Many felt that Broadbent had allowed Turner to seize the mantle of chief opponent to Mulroney's free trade proposal. After the election, Canadian Auto Workers leader Bob White wrote to Broadbent: "I can tell you that I've never seen such a level of disappointment and anger among our activists. There is a common thread in the frustration, and that is that the NDP, our party, never really came to grips with the importance of free trade."[12] Broadbent resigned as leader in 1989.

To replace him, the party chose Yukon MP Audrey McLaughlin, making her the first woman leader of a major Canadian federal party and an inspirational figure for showing that women can compete in politics on equal terms with men. Her victory was no cakewalk; she had to defeat Dave Barrett, former premier of British Columbia and a true party heavyweight. McLaughlin promised a "new politics," based on openness and consultation. The party's choice seemed inspired at first, as the NDP's standing rose in the polls. *Homemaker's* magazine gushed: "Her impish good looks are reminiscent of Audrey Hepburn, her political savvy of Margaret Thatcher and her listening skills of Lester Pearson. Those who do know her say Audrey McLaughlin is the political Messiah this country has been waiting for, the leader of the 90s."[13]

The honeymoon lasted a while. The party won provincial elections in Ontario, Saskatchewan, and British Columbia, creating the impression not just of an NDP wave but of a veritable tsunami. Instead of cresting, however, the tide quickly ran out. By supporting the Charlottetown Accord, the party alienated many of its working-class supporters, particularly in the West, where the new Reform Party provided competition as a populist party. The government of Bob Rae in Ontario, faced with a difficult financial situation, quickly became more of a liability than an asset to the NDP brand. The NDP's base of public sector unions did not take kindly to "Rae days" in Ontario – mandatory unpaid leave for public employees. And in Quebec, the Bloc siphoned off potential NDP supporters, who had always tended to flirt with separatism. Thus, when the election campaign began, the NDP was polling at about 10 percent and faced a fight for survival in a crowded marketplace of political protest.[14]

As a unified federal-provincial party, the NDP could always put together an experienced campaign team, drawing on veterans of provincial campaigns. The new leader was another matter, however. She was from Ontario but by way of Yukon, a remote and thinly populated part of Canada, so she did not have a large cadre of local supporters to fall back on. She spoke little French, which virtually ruled out making any gains in Quebec against native son francophones Lucien Bouchard and Jean Chrétien. Her appeal, moreover, was heavily based on feminism. The autobiography she published after becoming leader emphasized how she had overcome the obstacles to being a woman in public life.[15] The sardonic title, *A Woman's Place,* is indicative. It appealed to the progressives in the NDP, but the public at large seemed more concerned about rising unemployment and a stubbornly high federal deficit. After the initial novelty of being a female party leader wore off, McLaughlin came to be perceived, even within her own party, as a weak leader unable to pull the NDP out of its tailspin.

On the eve of the election, members of the NDP caucus were feuding in public with the leader and with each other. Things looked so bad that, at a secret meeting, McLaughlin offered to resign, but the party executive refused her offer.[16] Whatever was said in public, the real goal of party insiders was to win at least twelve seats and retain official party status in the House of Commons.[17] Shortly before the writ was dropped, word got out that director of communications Michael Balagus had an important video about McLaughlin edited in the United States, claiming he could not find an agency in Canada to do it in the allotted time. It became the biggest story of the year for the NDP because it undercut the party's claim to be opposed to free trade with our southern neighbour. Balagus resigned, and once again party officials and advisers were shuffled.[18]

Bloc Québécois

The Bloc was in a very favourable position at the start of the campaign. Lucien Bouchard had inspired defections from both the Conservatives and Liberals to create a Bloc Québécois caucus in the House of Commons. Gilles Duceppe, who won a by-election in 1990, strengthened the mix because his background as a union organizer was further to the left. Bouchard now led a trans-ideological party spanning the political spectrum from left to right, the chief unifying factor being a desire for Quebec independence.

The Bloc, therefore, took eclectic and sometimes contradictory positions. For example, it was in favour of reducing the federal deficit while also increasing social welfare expenditures.[19] But consistency didn't matter. Everyone knew that the real purpose of the Bloc was to represent the separatist cause in Ottawa, perhaps exercising leverage in Parliament if, as was then widely expected, the 1993 election produced a minority government.

When he first ran for office in 1988, Bouchard was a political novice who had to learn the basics of campaigning from Brian Mulroney. He evolved into a master campaigner in his own right, however. Highly educated and well read, he was also a passionate orator, bordering on the demagogic, not worried about the consistency that Ralph Waldo Emerson called "the hobgoblin of little minds." His biographer, *Globe and Mail* columnist Lawrence Martin, referred to his "politics of delusion,"[20] but he was no more delusional than most political leaders. He couldn't have founded a new political party, swept the province, and later become premier of Quebec without a strong grasp of political realities. Delusional, no – but the perfect leader to fan the embers of resentment into separatist flames.

The Bloc had a big strategic advantage in that it had to campaign in only one province. Bouchard could concentrate on Quebec while the leaders of the other parties had to criss-cross the country in search of votes. The party didn't have a lot of money, but that didn't matter because campaigning in one province was much cheaper than campaigning across the whole country. The party also didn't have much of a ground organization, but that didn't matter because Quebec premier Jacques Parizeau authorized the organization of the Parti Québécois to work for the Bloc. (Bouchard and Parizeau had a rather fraught personal relationship, but for the time being they kept it in the background for the sake of the greater cause.) With these advantages, and polling about 40 percent in Quebec on the eve of the election, the Bloc seemed a safe bet to win at least thirty or forty seats, perhaps more if the campaign flowed their way.

Liberal Party of Canada

The 1980s were a traumatic decade for the Liberals as they lost the elections of 1984 and 1988 under the leadership of John Turner.[21] Jean Chrétien, who had lost to Turner in the 1984 leadership race, won a new leadership race in 1990 after Turner resigned. This was actually just one episode in a generations-long struggle for control of the Liberal Party. One party insider has written a book of almost 700 pages titled *Divided Loyalties: The Liberal Party of Canada, 1984–2008,* and yet it tells only part of the story.[22]

Liberal leaders after the First World War – William Lyon Mackenzie King, Louis St. Laurent, and Lester Pearson – were all relatively unifying figures, useful for a party that covered a broad centrist spectrum. In 1968, Pierre Trudeau, who had previously been a member of the NDP, became the party's leader by defeating several business-oriented candidates, including John Turner. Turner served in a number of high-profile cabinet portfolios under Trudeau before decamping for Bay Street, where he devoted himself to planning to win the leadership one day.

That moment came in 1984 after Trudeau announced his retirement, and Turner defeated Jean Chrétien, who at the time approximately represented Trudeau's more leftist wing of the party. Turner's leadership was marked by a great degree of internal disunity, and after twice failing to lead the party to victory in a national election, his time was up. The mantle of business was picked up by the successful entrepreneur Paul Martin Jr., who, along with Sheila Copps, ran against Chrétien in 1990. Perhaps mindful of the adage that you should hold your friends close and your enemies closer, Chrétien made Copps deputy leader and Martin finance critic, a job for which he was well suited because of his extensive business background. The NDP and the Conservatives would have female leaders, and the Liberals would have a woman as deputy leader – another way in which 1993 was a landmark election.

Chrétien, Martin, and Copps managed to work together, but Martin was never really liked or trusted by the other two, particularly because he had supported the Meech Lake Accord and Chrétien, like Trudeau, had opposed it.[23] Copps also thought Martin was misusing his power as minister of finance to marginalize internal opponents and build support for a future leadership bid.[24] After Chrétien won a third straight majority government in 2000, Martin became impatient and finally rolled out his campaign to take over the party at the constituency level.[25] Faced with the probability of an unfavourable leadership review from delegates at a national convention, Chrétien announced his resignation. Martin then won a leadership race with little competition and became prime minister on December 12, 2003. Only Sheila Copps persevered to the end in her leadership campaign against overwhelming odds, for which Martin repaid her by keeping her out of cabinet and preventing her from being nominated again in 2004 in her riding of Hamilton East – Stoney Mountain.[26]

But in 1993 all that lay in the future, as Chrétien, Copps, and Martin kept their differences largely out of sight. Even so, prospects did not seem favourable at first for the new leader, who was widely panned for his folksy manner of expressing himself in both English and French. He then proceeded to make many enemies in Quebec and elsewhere for leading the Liberals in support of the Charlottetown Accord during the 1992 referendum.

Yet Chrétien, who had first been elected to Parliament in 1963, had three decades of political experience to draw on. He methodically set about rebuilding the Liberal Party and getting ready for the next election. He recruited a competent team around himself. He dealt with the party's considerable debt by improving corporate fundraising. He also tackled the issue of candidate recruitment, centralizing the process so he could have more female candidates as well as those who appealed to specific ethnic communities, and "stars" who might be ready for a cabinet position immediately upon wining power. He pushed through rules that allowed the leader not only to reject candidates but also to appoint candidates without a nomination contest. There had been many bruising nomination battles in the Turner years, which Chrétien hoped to avoid. The new rules were controversial within the party but did in fact produce a team of candidates, including not only more women but also well-known cabinet material such as Allan Rock, Art Eggleton, and Marcel Massé, who had not previously run for the Liberals.[27]

Perhaps most importantly, he undertook the intellectual rejuvenation of the party. A widely publicized thinkers' conference held at Aylmer, Quebec, in 1991 helped the party come to terms with free trade, which the Liberals had opposed so strenuously in the 1988 election. After the conference, Chrétien authorized a committee chaired by Chaviva Hošek and Paul Martin to draft *Creating Opportunity: The Liberal Plan for Canada*, commonly known as the Red Book, the Liberal platform for the coming campaign. Hošek, who had had electoral experience in Ontario politics, was now director of the Liberal caucus research bureau. Martin conceived the idea of the Red Book and was the driving force behind its creation. Chrétien was happy to let him do the job. He intervened only to rein in Martin's enthusiasm for balancing the budget, imposing instead a deficit target of 3 percent of gross domestic product.[28]

Written platforms had gone out of fashion in Canadian politics, replaced by leaders' serial policy announcements during the course of the campaign. But voters were ready for more stability after years of the Mulroney government's introduction of policies, such as free trade and the GST, on which it had not campaigned. Having a written platform was a particularly good idea for Jean Chrétien, who, in spite of his many other political abilities, lacked verbal agility. Now, when questioned about policy issues, he could point to the Red Book and say, "It's all in here."[29]

Despite Chrétien's perceived image problems, the Liberals led in the polls in the early 1990s. It was a time of economic recession and high unemployment, which generally cause voters to start considering the suitability of the opposition party as a government. Also, the debacle of the Charlottetown Accord had driven many erstwhile Conservative supporters to the new BQ and Reform options. But the Liberals suffered a scare when the Conservatives chose Kim Campbell as their new leader. Besides being the first woman to lead Sir John A. Macdonald's party, she seemed to have some advantages over Chrétien, being younger and more articulate. As Conservative support rebounded and Campbell's personal approval numbers soared in public polls, Chrétien drew on his long experience to calm the "nervous Nellies" in his caucus.[30]

When the election kicked off in early September, the Liberals still appeared to be the favourites, but not by very much. Both the Liberals and the Conservatives were in the low thirties in most public opinion polls, but the Conservatives' position was fragile because of the threat posed by the BQ and Reform to their two pillars of Quebec and the West. They would need an outstanding campaign to hold their renewed support and finish first, whereas Chrétien needed only to look experienced, calm, and well prepared in order to hold on to Liberal support. In the event, the Conservatives would become ensnared in a disastrous campaign, and Chrétien's Liberals would cruise to a majority government.

Progressive Conservative Party

Initially, Kim Campbell's selection as the new leader seemed to have restored the Progressive Conservatives' competitiveness. In the last two years of Brian Mulroney's leadership, they had been polling at around 20 percent, sometimes even lower. It was not just the gruelling constitutional debate; the early 1990s were a time of recession, job losses, acrimony over the GST, and growing government deficits. After rejecting the Charlottetown Accord, voters had turned their attention to the economy, looking for good news or at least signs of hope from the party leaders.

Kim Campbell at first seemed to be what they wanted. Her polling numbers started high when she announced her run for the leadership, declined during that campaign, but rose again after she won and took over the reins of government. A confidential August 1993 poll by Decima Research had the Conservatives leading the Liberals nationally, 35 percent to 29 percent. The PCs, moreover, were running first, tied, or a close second in every region of the country, albeit against different opponents. They were tied with the Bloc in Quebec, two points behind the Liberals in Ontario, and one point behind the Liberals in British Columbia. Campbell's leadership approval score was twenty points ahead of Chrétien's at the national level.[31] With those numbers, an election seemed like a good bet. In theory, Campbell's high leadership approval should have enabled her to swing close races towards the Conservatives.

A potential weakness was waiting to show itself, however. Campbell had made her leadership campaign mainly about herself. She would do politics differently. She would listen to and engage in dialogue with voters. She was not Mulroney – and yet all the while she remained a minister in Mulroney's cabinet. So how different could she really be if she was still part of the old government? Campbell later wrote: "I made many mistakes in the campaigns and other events of 1993, but I think the greatest one may have been not to call the PM's bluff and resign from cabinet."[32]

Not surprisingly, Campbell never produced a clear policy profile for herself during the leadership campaign, nor did she fill the void after she became prime minister. A decision was made over the summer of 1993 not to prepare a campaign platform but to release policy in a series of speeches by the leader. The Conservatives thought that without a platform they would be free to criticize and attack the Liberals' Red Book while remaining more flexible themselves.[33] They wanted the campaign to be about leadership, not about the details of policy. It might have worked with a more disciplined leader, but Campbell, to show she was doing politics differently, spoke at length in meetings and interviews, and she sometimes said things that could be taken out of context and used against her. Without a written platform to structure her statements and refer to for clarification, she was in hot water from the beginning of the campaign, not least due to things she had said in the leadership campaign.

One example: at a Conservative leadership debate on May 13, she called those who denied that the deficit was a problem "enemies of Canadians." It was an unfortunate echo of Brian Mulroney's famous charge that those who opposed the Charlottetown Accord were "enemies of Canada." Campbell later said she had meant to say "adversaries," but "enemies" slipped out and the damage was done.[34] As most Canadian politicians realize, "enemies" is a word best left to warfare and kept out of domestic politics.

Another example: on May 18, the *Toronto Star* ran a report that "Kim Campbell says she got converted Anglican to ward off the evil demons of the papacy." The story turned out to have come from an earlier interview Campbell had done with the journalist Peter C. Newman, in which she had discussed her attendance at a Catholic girls' school: "When I went to St. Anne's ... it was pre-Vatican II days. The nuns still wore habits, the mass in Latin, and I got confirmed an Anglican the year I was there, I suppose as a way of warding off the evil demons of the papacy or whatever."[35] It should have been obvious to any fair-minded reader that in the Newman interview Campbell was making an ironic, self-deprecating comment about another time and place. Yet, sadly, politicians have to learn the danger of humour. What may seem funny in one context does not always travel well.

By staying so long in office, Mulroney did not leave much time for his successor to develop her own profile and her own campaign team. Campbell wasn't sworn in as prime minister until June 25, and an election had to be held no later than October 25, with a campaign launch in early September if the voter enumeration carried out for the Charlottetown Accord referendum was to be used. This wasn't a legal requirement, but the expense of conducting another enumeration would have become a campaign issue in its own right if Campbell had delayed calling an election. Yet ten weeks from late June to early September was little time to prepare for a national campaign. You can put some of the mechanisms in place in a couple of months, but you can't develop policy and thoroughly road-test it with the public. The Conservative Party of Canada would be placed in a similar position in spring 2004, when Stephen Harper won the leadership on March 20 and Liberal prime minister Paul Martin started the election campaign on May 23. Both in 1993 and in 2004, the short lead time made it difficult for the campaign team to test its platform and produce effective advertising.[36]

Under the circumstances, Campbell decided to rely on Mulroney's campaign team, which had won national electoral victories for the Conservatives in 1984 and 1988. The two key figures were pollster Allan Gregg (Decima Research) and manager John Tory, who was elected mayor of Toronto in 2015 after a losing turn as leader of the Ontario Progressive Conservatives. They would run campaign headquarters in Toronto while Campbell was out on tour. But thorny problems of communication can arise between campaign HQ and the tour team, and these are exacerbated when the leader and the campaign manager barely know each other and are not used to working together. This communication gap ultimately drove the PC campaign from unsuccessful to catastrophic. The campaign team inherited from Mulroney had a track record of success, but even the best team cannot win if it is not in sync with the leader.

Money

It costs money to maintain a political party and run an election campaign. No campaign manager would ever ask for less money, because you can always run more ads, hold more rallies, or do more polling. Indeed, money is sometimes the decisive factor in a campaign, as in the 1988 federal election. Liberal leader John Turner caused his party's support to jump ahead by attacking Mulroney over the Free Trade Agreement with the United States in the leaders' debate, telling him, "You sold us out." The Conservatives responded with an expensive negative ad campaign directed at Turner. The most memorable line came from a supposed ordinary voter saying about Turner, "He's out to save his job, not mine."[37] Polling results suggest that the ads turned back the Liberal surge and led to the ultimate Conservative victory. Without their financial resources, the Conservatives could not have afforded such expensive tactics in 1988. Money does not seem to have been a decisive factor in the 1993 election, however.

Table 3.1 shows the money spent by the major parties during the 1993 election campaign. Expenditure totals are in 1993 dollars. The cost of living increased about 60 percent from 1993 to 2020, so the purchasing power of those expenditures in 1993 was much greater than it would be today.

Bear in mind that these figures refer to the spending of the national campaign. Under Canadian law, each candidate has a campaign budget for expenses in the local riding, whereas the party has a separate national budget. For each of the main parties except for the NDP, the total of candidate spending in 1993 was larger than that of the national campaign.[38] Also, the party has ongoing expenses that are necessary to the national campaign even if they are not counted as campaign expenses. These categories are not watertight

TABLE 3.1

National campaign spending, 1993 general election

Party	Total expenditure ($)	Votes received	Expenditure per vote ($)
PC	10,400,000	2,186,422	4.76
Liberal	9,900,000	5,647,952	1.75
NDP	7,400,000	939,975	7.87
Reform	1,500,000	2,559,245	0.59
BQ	1,900,000	1,846,244	1.03

Sources: Expenditure totals are compiled from Elections Canada, *Thirty-Fifth General Election, 1993: Contributions and Expenses of Registered Political Parties and Candidates* (Ottawa: Chief Electoral Officer of Canada, 1993), 23, Table 6. Vote totals are from Wikipedia, s.v. "1993 Canadian federal election," last modified April 22, 2022, https://en.wikipedia.org/wiki/1993_Canadian_federal_election.

Note: Expenditures are rounded to the nearest hundred thousand. The totals are not available on the Elections Canada website, which contains data going back only to 1997.

compartments, so money moves around to some extent throughout the party structure, the national campaign, and the local campaigns. However, Elections Canada enforces an elaborate set of rules that are the same for all, so the totals reported here are a good indication of the relative spending of the parties.

The second column in Table 3.1 shows the number of votes received by each party, and the third column presents a dollars-per-vote calculation (first column divided by the second column). Dollars per vote is a frequently used indicator of the efficiency of campaign spending viewed as a means of attracting popular support. In some ways, dollars per seat won would be a better indicator of efficiency, because seats are what really count at the end of the day. However, its interpretation is more complex because it also depends upon how other parties deployed their own expenditures. For this reason, we use dollars per vote here.

With these preliminaries out of the way, let's take a closer look at the parties. The Conservatives were the biggest spenders, though their margin over the Liberals was only half a million dollars. However, the Liberals got more "bang for the buck" than the Tories –

TABLE 3.2

Fundraising by Canadian political parties, 1993 ($)

Party	Total	Average contribution
PC	22,300,000	416
Liberal	14,700,000	302
NDP	9,100,000	136
Reform	7,100,000	139

Source: Compiled from Elections Canada, *Thirty-Fifth General Election, 1993: Contributions and Expenses of Registered Political Parties and Candidates* (Ottawa: Chief Electoral Officer of Canada, 1993), 5, Table 1.

Note: Contribution totals are rounded to the nearest hundred thousand. Data for the Bloc Québécois are not included in the source.

$1.75 versus $4.76 per vote – because their messaging resonated better. Both Reform and the BQ, each appealing in its own way to a subset of the national electorate, were more efficient spenders than the two big parties. The NDP was the least efficient spender of all because it had geared up to run a full-scale national campaign, hoping to win government or at least become the official opposition, but finished a poor fifth. Both the PC and NDP examples show that spending large amounts of money will not save you if your message does not connect with voters.

Table 3.2 shows the fundraising totals for national parties in the 1993 calendar year, which includes the writ period of the election campaign.

Historically, the PCs and Liberals had depended chiefly on corporate and large individual donations. An old-time fundraiser once told me what it was like for both parties in the 1950s. You went to head offices in Toronto and Montreal, he said, and it was over in a few days. Of course, that's an exaggeration, like all such stories, but it does capture a large part of the way things used to be.

The Conservatives moved into the lead in the 1970s when party director John Laschinger began using database-linked direct mail as a fundraising technique.[39] Their earlier deployment of mass fundraising techniques gave the PCs an edge that helped them win in 1984 and 1988. As always happens in politics, the Liberals saw the effect of what their opponents were doing and took steps to catch up, but they were still behind the PCs in 1993 –$14.7 million compared with $22.3 million. However, they were able to borrow money from Canadian banks to more or less match the PCs in campaign spending.

It is noteworthy that the Liberals and Conservatives got about 60 percent of their money from corporations, while the NDP got about a third of its cash from labour unions.[40] Certain large expenses in campaigns, such as payment for advertising time, occur early in the campaign. Based on many bad experiences in the past, advertisers and other suppliers are reluctant to extend credit during campaigns, so parties have to pay in advance. Corporate, union, and other large donations, all of which are now illegal but were legal in 1993, could be gathered early to help pay for these up-front expenses. They also gave comfort to banks, which would make loans to political parties if they were satisfied about the chances of repayment. Grassroots fundraising from small donors can raise a lot of money during the campaign as voter enthusiasm grows, but the money tends to come in too late to cover advertising time and other up-front expenses. This was especially relevant in the case of the Reform Party.

Because Reform spent less than $2 million in the 1993 campaign, it was playing in the minor financial leagues compared with the three old-line parties. Only 12 percent of its money came from corporations, and these donors were mostly smaller companies owned by individuals and families. The corporate giants at this time supported the Liberals and Conservatives, period. Nor did unions contribute to Reform, though some of their members did. Reform, therefore, had to support itself through grassroots fundraising, mainly from party members. Not surprisingly, banks were not eager to lend to Reform, nor did the party want to take out big bank loans;

its strong critique of public debt made it averse to taking on debt for its own operations. Bereft of corporate and union support, big donors, and bank loans, Reform could afford only a minimum of TV advertising, using mainly the free time provided as a public service by the networks. Operating largely without paid media, Reform had to rely on the earned media, that is, news coverage that came from interviews and rallies, particularly Preston Manning's appearances at such events.

PULLING TOGETHER ALL this information about the organizational and financial assets of the parties, the most plausible prediction before the campaign would have been that the Liberals and Conservatives would wage a fairly close contest for power, and the victor might well have to be satisfied with a minority government, since both parties were polling in the lower 30 percent range, traditional minority government territory. The BQ appeared certain to win a large number of seats in francophone Quebec, while Reform might pick up some seats in the West, and the NDP would get a few here and there – all of which might make it difficult for either the Liberals or Conservatives to assemble enough seats for a majority. Thus the leaders of the three smaller parties could dream of holding the balance of power, depending on how things turned out.

In fact, things turned out in a way that no one had anticipated, allowing the Liberals to sweep to a majority government while the PCs collapsed and the BQ and Reform won large numbers of seats in their regional strongholds. It's like the Grey Cup or Super Bowl. Teams may look well matched on paper, leading to forecasts of a close game, but sometimes one team wins a lopsided victory. The game matters; that's why we play it. Similarly, campaigns matter, and in 1993 the course of the campaign would be decisive.

4

The Contest

AN OVERVIEW OF how the parties fared in public opinion polls from early 1993 until just before voting day, October 25, is shown in Figure 4.1. The main drama was provided by the duel between the Liberals and Progressive Conservatives (top two lines). The Liberals were far ahead early in the year as the Conservatives still suffered from the referendum defeat of the Charlottetown Accord, the public relations fiasco of the GST, and Brian Mulroney's general unpopularity. Then the gap gradually closed as Mulroney announced his retirement on February 24, 1993, and Kim Campbell won the resulting leadership race and was sworn in as prime minister on June 25. By the time the election was called on September 8, the two parties seemed to be in a dead heat, which continued for about two weeks until the roof fell in on the Tories. In this chapter, we examine in more detail the campaign, or "writ period," as political observers often call it, from September 8 through October 25, 1993.

At one level, the story of the 1993 campaign is very simple. The Progressive Conservatives started more or less even with the Liberals, in the range of 30–35 percent of decided voters, as reported in various polls. This rough tie continued for the first two weeks, then the PCs began trending remorselessly downward, eventually

FIGURE 4.1
Results of 1993 public opinion polls

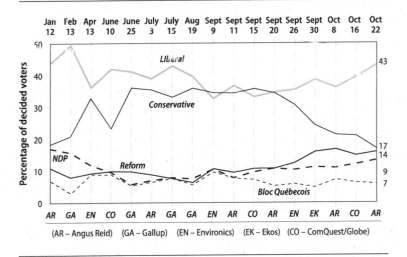

Source: Adapted from Tom Flanagan, *Waiting for the Wave: The Reform Party and the Conservative Movement* (Montreal and Kingston: McGill-Queen's University Press, 2009). Data from Canadian Press and *Globe and Mail*.

Note: Percentages for parties have been calculated without including undecided voters.

reaching the unprecedentedly low level of 16 percent of votes on election day. Meanwhile, the Liberals, the Reform Party, and the Bloc Québécois all climbed upward. The Liberals ended up with a majority government, the BQ became the official opposition, and Reform won more seats than most pundits thought possible. The NDP chugged along at 10 percent or less in the polls and was never much of a factor in the campaign.

The above paragraph describes the campaign in cold, dispassionate terms. In fact, however, the central narrative of the campaign was the moving and sad human story of how the PCs and their new leader fumbled away the progress they appeared to have made after replacing Brian Mulroney with Kim Campbell. The other parties surged by reacting to the steady stream of Conservative errors resulting from the structural factors previously discussed –

lack of a campaign platform, lack of mutual understanding between the leader's tour and campaign headquarters, a leader determined to "do politics differently" without fully understanding the dangers that would bring. For political observers, it became a clinical study in how not to run a campaign.

Conservative problems manifested themselves on September 8, the very first day of the campaign. After the traditional visit to Governor General Ray Hnatyshyn to request a dissolution of Parliament, Prime Minister Campbell gave a speech followed by a press conference. The speech identified unemployment and the deficit as her two main priorities, which was in line with public opinion. In the Canadian National Election Study, 43 percent of respondents identified unemployment as their main concern, while 14 percent mentioned the deficit and another 6 percent mentioned the closely allied issue of taxes.[1]

Campbell got the issues right: both unemployment and deficit spending had been rising since 1990. However, she provided little if any detail as to what she planned to do about them. When quizzed on jobs during the press conference, she said that Canada would continue to suffer high unemployment "for the next two, three or four years," but that by "the turn of the century," unemployment in Canada would be "way down."[2] The statement might have been fine in a university seminar but could easily be spun against her by election opponents. If she had stuck to the message of her speech, she would have been safe, but she improvised and amplified it in the question period.

It was a godsend to the Liberals. Their Red Book made jobs a priority, to be delivered by a major infrastructure program. Granted, the program couldn't be financed without going further into debt, and infrastructure programs often don't deliver the promised boost to employment because of inevitable delays in getting money out the door. But all that was beside the point in campaign rhetoric. Jean Chrétien had a program, whereas Campbell appeared to be putting nothing on the table, saying voters would just have to wait for years for there to be any improvement. The Liberals easily caricatured her position as heartless and indifferent.

In spite of the opening-day gaffe and some rather sloppily organized events in the following days, Conservative support initially held up well. A poll released after the first week showed the Conservatives with 36 percent of decided voters against the Liberals with 33 percent.[3] The BQ was in first place in Quebec at 40 percent, but the PCs were second with 32 percent, and the Liberals were a distant third there with 20 percent of decided voters. As a former campaign manager, I've been in the same situation. You know your campaign isn't executing well, but your voter support seems to be stable. You pray for the miracle to last, but it never does. There may be some time delay, but fundamentally weak campaigns break down sooner or later.

The Liberals released the Red Book on September 12. The contrast with the Conservatives, who had not planned to have a formal platform, was damaging. The Conservatives hastily put together a platform, titled *The Taxpayers' Agenda,* and released it thirteen days later, but it had little effect because it looked like a rushed response.[4] The delay in preparing and releasing a platform not only made the Conservatives look bad compared with the Liberals but also sabotaged other aspects of the Conservative campaign. One of the main functions of a platform is to provide structure to the leader's statements, and without that discipline Campbell tended to wander when she spoke.

Ideally, the platform should be prepared, though held closely confidential, months or at least weeks before the campaign. The platform then becomes the guide for scripting the campaign, including the talking points for the "message of the day," the travel plan for the leader's tour, and the media buy for advertising.[5] Improvisation may be fine for a certain kind of comedy, but it is disastrous for a modern political campaign, in which the media and the opponent's war room are watching all the time and ready to pounce on any misstep.

The wheels fell off the Conservative campaign on day 16. Kim Campbell later wrote: "If there is one day in the campaign that I would like to write off the calendar, it would be September 23, 1993."[6] That morning, the *Globe and Mail* ran a front-page story claiming a secret government document showed that the Conservatives were planning to make cuts to social programs in order to eliminate the deficit in five years, as Campbell had promised. In a scrum with reporters, Campbell was asked about the alleged plan. She replied: "The first budget of the new government would be in February of '94, and Parliament will come back this fall – I think there is ample opportunity to engage Canadians in a serious dialogue and to work with the provinces to find the best way to deliver those services." When asked why she wasn't discussing these issues during the election campaign, she replied with the fatal sentence: "I think that's the worst possible time to have that kind of dialogue." Then she dug herself in even more deeply: "The issues are much too complex to try and generate some kind of blueprint in the forty-seven days that's available in an election campaign," and "this is not the time, I don't think, to get involved in a debate on very, very serious issues."[7]

One could distill a sensible position from Campbell's statements, something along the lines of, "these are complex issues, the provinces are involved, if we are re-elected we will discuss them methodically with the public and the provinces, etc." But in the heat of a campaign, her exchange with reporters provided a bonanza of short clips for her opponents to use against her, to allege that she had a secret plan and was contemptuous of the public's intelligence. The next day's headlines were devastating: "'Election not time to debate cuts: PM,' went the *Toronto Star*. 'PM won't touch key issues,' said the *Globe and Mail*. 'Now's not time for issues, PM says,' repeated the *Ottawa Citizen*."[8]

Conservative support started sliding at this moment and never recovered. The PCs had been tied with the Liberals in an Angus Reid poll on September 20. By September 26, the Liberals had a five- or seven-point lead, depending on which poll results you believed.[9] And things never got better. To quote the title of a Bruce Springsteen song, the Conservative campaign had become a "downbound train," on which nothing went right. Campbell tried to stem the damage with a speech on her budgetary plans, but an editorial board meeting with the *Globe and Mail* did still more harm. "Yesterday afternoon," wrote the *Globe*, "a day after she delivered her long-awaited plan, she was still struggling to make sense of it."[10]

The damage was compounded by Preston Manning's re-release of his Zero in Three plan on September 20. Previously, the Reform campaign had been in a "Let the People Speak" phase, in which Manning turned over the microphone to members of the audience at campaign rallies. He said on opening day: "In this election, don't let anyone else tell you what the agenda is. This time *you* tell the oldline politicians what is important and what is not. *You* tell the oldline politicians what is good for us and what is not. *You* tell the oldine politicians what they can do with their political correctness."[11]

This populist ploy seemed to have little impact on voters as Reform's polling support remained stuck in the range of 10–12 percent, but Zero in Three sparked more interest. Remarkably, the *Globe and Mail* quickly endorsed it: "Reform is the one party to date to trust Canadians with the truth."[12] Manning had released the plan the previous spring with little impact, but the media seemed to have forgotten that early release and now treated it as a new announcement. Thus Reform began attracting attention for its budget-balancing plan just as the media were eviscerating Campbell for lacking a plan. To be sure, more voters considered unemployment a higher priority than the deficit, but those who did care about the deficit suddenly had a new alternative. Reform was still languishing at around 10 percent in the polls on September 20 but began tracking upward thereafter, due to the simple clarity of Zero in Three compared with Campbell's flailing confusion over the deficit.

The last real chance for the Conservatives to turn things around was the leaders' debates, scheduled for October 3 in French and the next day in English. Campbell set aside three days for preparation, which should have been more than adequate, but she did not hold the usual type of rehearsal, a mock debate in which suitable team members play the role of other leaders.[13] Debate rehearsal is indeed one of the most difficult things a leader has to do. Like many leaders, Campbell was reluctant to perform this way in front of her staff, but events would show that she might have benefited from going through the ordeal. In one poll that evaluated voters' overall judgment of both debates, she was ranked fourth out of the five leaders, ahead of only Audrey McLaughlin. Only 9 percent of respondents thought she had "won" the English-language debate, compared with 36 percent for Chrétien.[14]

A pivotal exchange occurred in the English debate, when Lucien Bouchard blindsided Campbell with questions about the size of the federal deficit. As recounted by political scientist Lawrence LeDuc:

"I had a question. It is a simple figure. What is the real deficit?" he [Bouchard] demanded. Campbell forged on. "I have a plan to eliminate the deficit." Bouchard: "You are hiding the truth, madam. You don't answer the question." "What is the alternative?" continued Campbell, not acknowledging Bouchard's interventions. "There is no alternative to the truth," Bouchard shot back.[15]

Technically, Bouchard's line of questioning was unfair because this was October 1993 and the exact size of the deficit would not be known until months after the end of the fiscal year in April

1994.[16] But politics is not about fairness; it is more like theatre, and Bouchard's theatrics were devastating to Campbell's claim to be a deficit fighter. How could you lead a war against the deficit if you could not even say how large it was?

Admittedly, Campbell faced a formidable challenge because at that point in the campaign, the Conservatives were bleeding support in all directions – to Reform in the West, the Liberals in Ontario and Atlantic Canada, and the Bloc in Quebec. Against the Liberals and Reform, she tried to position herself in the centre, saying she was the only leader interested in both creating jobs and cutting the deficit. In contrast, she said, Chrétien cared only about his unaffordable infrastructure plan, while Manning's obsession with balancing the budget showed his lack of compassion for the unemployed. But her attempt to straddle the issues failed to generate fresh support. Against Bouchard, Campbell tried to use an old quote from former Parti Québécois leader and Quebec premier René Lévesque, who had died in 1985. Lévesque had said that separatist leaders belonged in Quebec City and had no business running for office in Ottawa. But Bouchard hit back with a reply that worked for his Quebec audience: "You have no business raking over the ashes of René Lévesque."[17]

After the debates, the Conservative campaign continued its downward spiral, reaching polling numbers of around 20 percent in the first half of October. This would have handed the PCs a historic defeat, but it would probably have given them at least the twelve seats they needed to be a recognized party in the House of Commons. Conservative strategists made things worse, however, in trying to turn the tide with a desperate last advertising release.

The final collapse was precipitated by a pair of English television ads released on October 15, day 38 of the campaign.[18] They were thirty-second spots questioning Chrétien's ability to be prime minister because he didn't understand the economics of deficits, debt, infrastructure, and unemployment. The text was hard-hitting

Jean Chrétien's partial facial paralysis
was due to Bell's palsy. | Fred Chartrand,
The Canadian Press

but hardly unprecedented. What made the ads controversial was
that the visuals consisted of a series of close-up photographs of
Chrétien's face, showing the somewhat twisted expression resulting from the Bell's palsy that had afflicted him since youth. In that
context, the final words of the ads, "Jean Chrétien a prime minister?
Think twice," could be taken as a comment on his appearance as
well as his policies.

The ads had been prepared by the brain trust at campaign headquarters, primarily pollster Allan Gregg and advertising coordinator
Tom Scott; Campbell had never seen them and didn't know anything
about them. That in itself seems extraordinary. In most campaigns,
the team would never dream of releasing an ad for national television

without running it by the leader. That this occurred shows how bad communication between the Tory war room and the leader's tour had become.

The ads had been tested on focus groups without setting off alarm bells, but their release precipitated a firestorm in public opinion.[19] Most damaging was that many Conservative candidates and party officials publicly condemned them. Nothing is more lethal to a campaign than the public airing of disagreement by members of the campaign team. Also, the Liberals contacted organizations representing the handicapped and urged them to make protest calls to Conservative campaign offices. Jean Chrétien replied both cleverly and movingly: "They try to make fun of the way I look. God gave me a physical defect and I've accepted that since I was a kid."[20] Campbell ordered the ad withdrawn, but her graceless apology to Chrétien probably did more harm than good: "If Mr. Chrétien or any others have been offended in any way ..."[21]

After this debacle, Campbell continued to campaign hard but nothing went right. In a meeting with the editorial board of *La Presse*, she made disparaging remarks about Brian Mulroney, Jean Charest, and former finance minister Don Mazankowski. Charest, she said, did not have a "fleshed out" vision, while Mazankowski had taken "too much of an accounting approach" to deficit reduction. About Mulroney she said, "I believe that during the last eight years, we have done things in a way that did not work, that sapped the credibility of the political process ... a lot of things were done in a way that I would not have done."[22] She should have distanced herself from Mulroney much earlier if she was going to do it at all. At this point in the campaign, her remarks sounded offensive and provoked a public feud with one of her Quebec cabinet colleagues, Jean Corbeil, resulting in another climb-down and semi-apology.

In the final days, Campbell continued to tour the country, but the closing Conservative message may have made a bad situation even worse, if that was possible. She emphasized that a strong majority government was necessary to beat back the regionally based assaults from Reform and the Bloc. But anyone paying attention to her and thinking seriously about polling results at that point would have had to conclude that only the Liberals had a chance of forming a strong majority government – as indeed happened. The Conservative message may have had merit, but the timing was completely wrong.

Meanwhile Reform had not done anything spectacular since releasing Zero in Three. Lacking money, its underfunded advertising campaign was minimal and probably moved few if any votes, but at least it avoided dramatic errors like fiasco of the Tories' anti-Chrétien attack ads. Unable to afford significant advertising, the campaign distributed over 19 million pieces of literature.[23] Lack of money also forced Reform's leader's tour to be low-key. Manning and his small team of aides travelled by commercial airline until the last week of the campaign because the party could not afford to charter a jet. But again the party managed to avoid the kind of tour-related episode that can do so much damage, like Robert Stanfield's dropped football in 1974 or Joe Clark's lost luggage on a foreign tour (though he recovered from that to win the 1979 election).[24]

With its strong position on balanced budgets, Reform benefited from the Conservative death spiral, peaking at about 20 percent of national support in mid-October, then trailing off a bit in the final weeks. In his memoirs, Manning blamed the John Beck episode for the late slide. Beck, a member of the Toronto taxi-owning family, was the Reform candidate in York Centre, a very weak riding for the party. He had been nominated by a vote of fourteen out of the twenty-three people who attended the constituency nomination meeting.[25] Apparently, he concealed his true views when filling out the candidate questionnaire and going through the compulsory interview. I have heard Reform veterans say Beck was a plant from another party but have never seen actual evidence of this. A plant would make a great episode in a political novel, but a university press book has to stick to the evidence.

On October 13, Manning was confronted with a recent statement of Beck's: "I feel the time has come for white Anglo-Saxons to get involved ... We're destroying ourselves hourly ... and the people [immigrants] coming from another country, one evil is just as bad as another."[26] Beck was quickly forced to resign from his candidacy, but the episode received wide play in the Ontario media and led to scrutiny of other questionable comments by Reform candidates. Manning later wrote that the bad publicity cost Reform several seats in Ontario, which, had they been won, would have made the party the official opposition after the election and also given it a more national and less regional image.[27] With so many things going on simultaneously, it is difficult to attribute causality to one episode, but the Beck affair certainly didn't help Reform's push for votes in Ontario. Reform had to be content with third-party rather than official-opposition status and was forever branded as a Western regional party. Reform, one might say, exceeded initial expectations but did not fulfill its highest hopes.

In some ways, the Bloc Québécois campaign was similar to that of Reform. For the first two weeks, the Bloc stayed steady at its "cruising speed" of about 40 percent support in Quebec,[28] a level it had achieved long before the election, then it began rising in the polls as Conservative support disintegrated. But there was no last-minute decline of the type that Reform experienced, just a steady climb to reach 50 percent in the final week.

Bouchard made no Campbell-style gaffes to alienate voters, nor were there Reform-style "bozo eruptions" among the party's candidates.[29] Bouchard turned in an impressive performance in the French debate, reassuring Quebec voters that he could be an effective premier if he later decided to move to provincial politics. The BQ platform cut across the ideological spectrum, agreeing with the Tories on free trade but tending more to the left on social policy, thus enabling francophone voters of all stripes to rally to the nationalist cause. Bouchard even persuaded about 10 percent of English voters in Quebec to cast their ballots for the Bloc.[30]

Bouchard barnstormed across Quebec with his passion not much constrained by facts. He blamed "the English people" for Canada's alarming debt and deficit. "We let them run Canada and now we have a country on the verge of bankruptcy,"[31] he said, ignoring the fact that the prime minister had been a Quebecer ever since 1968, except for the brief Clark interlude and the recent arrival of Campbell, and the fact that federal government spending had spiralled out of control under Pierre Trudeau. He also depicted Quebec as a loser in the game of federal fiscal transfers, although it was as obvious then as it is now that Quebec benefits hugely from programs such as equalization, supply management of dairy products, and federal support for science, culture, and higher education.[32] But he was speaking to an audience willing to believe, and he did not have to worry about fact-checkers in the rest of Canada, who would have gone unheard in Quebec anyway.

The NDP was never a major factor in the 1993 election campaign. According to insider Ian McLeod, internal dissension among caucus, staff, and senior volunteers resulted in a lack of strategic direction. They had trouble deciding what their main campaign theme would be (they finally settled on job creation) or who their main opponents were. Were they running against the Tories or the Liberals? Were they running to win the election, as they had hoped to do in 1988, or was their real objective to push the Liberals leftward? They largely ignored Reform, even though in the end Reform would take away many of their seats in the West.[33]

They had plenty of money for advertising, but their ads were ineffective. The first set, called "Angry Voices," was shot "in stark black and white and featured enraged Canadians shouting about various problems and governmental misdeeds."[34] The ads were pulled after a week when polling data from British Columbia suggested they were driving voters to Reform, not the NDP, but no effective replacements were designed. The NDP's number of targeted seats declined steadily over time, and by the end they were running a "save the furniture" campaign,[35] desperately trying to rescue a few of their best-known members from defeat. They ultimately elected nine MPs, not enough to be a recognized party in the House of Commons but sufficient to carry on while waiting for better days. At least they survived.

Ian McLeod summarized the campaign thus:

> The NDP, praying for voter volatility, started the campaign at 8 per cent, peaked at 10 in the second week, and then trailed off to 7. Only 4 per cent of Canadians wanted to see Audrey McLaughlin become prime minister, compared with 3 per cent for Mel Hurtig of the upstart National Party. The NDP's miraculously full slate of candidates included 110 women, a Canadian record, but this achievement generated hardly a ripple. The tour introduced some "new politics," in the form of McLaughlin meeting at round tables with ordinary folks, but the media ignored it. Instead they wrote portraits of the leader's dignity among the ruins.[36]

The Liberals were the greatest beneficiaries of the Conservative collapse. After September 23, their polling numbers rose steadily from the low to mid-30s to the low 40s, enough for a majority government, given the collapse of the PCs and NDP and the regional character of Reform and the BQ. The Liberals didn't have to do anything particularly brilliant to harvest these additional votes, just talk about infrastructure and jobs, act like the only truly national party, and point to the Red Book to deflect questions about policy. Chrétien's response to the Conservatives' "face ads" was an inspired piece of political ju-jitsu that probably helped the party take some additional seats, but by then the Liberals had already won the race.

Indeed, the Liberal campaign was smooth and well organized. *Globe and Mail* columnist and author Lawrence Martin later described it through the eyes of Liberal senator and campaign operative Joyce Fairbairn: "Never had she seen the level of preparedness she did for this campaign. They had the 112-page policy book; they had the trains, buses, and planes running on time; they had a well-rested leader with low expectations in a blue denim shirt."[37] They also had a quick-response war room modelled on what James Carville had invented for Bill Clinton in 1992.[38] They were ready to fire back quickly at Campbell, whatever she might say. For example, when the Conservatives unveiled their campaign slogan, "It's time," Chrétien was briefed to be on TV the same night, saying, "It's a fantastic slogan. Yes, it's time for a change. It's time to get the truth. It's time to throw them out."[39]

According to scholars, the Liberals were the only party to benefit from their own advertising campaign:

> Most ads featured Chrétien in a relaxed setting, a sunny room, talking informally and sincerely about problems of unemployment and job creation: for example, "Enough is enough. The Liberal Party has the plan to create jobs and can give back dignity to the unemployed," followed by a tagline "I have the people, I have the plan. We will make a difference," which ended almost all Liberal ads.[40]

Another effective move by the Liberals was to have Chrétien promise that he would not reopen the constitutional debate during his time in office.[41] More than anything else in the Mulroney years, the struggles over the Meech Lake and Charlottetown Accords had raised the temperature of politics. Now the Liberals were promising a time of renewed tranquility.

And then there was the Red Book's popular promise to "replace the GST with a system that generates equivalent revenues, is fairer to consumers and to small business, minimizes disruption to small business, and promotes federal-provincial fiscal co-operation and harmonization"[42] – a classic example of calculated ambiguity. Most voters probably thought it meant the GST would be cancelled, but what actually happened once the Liberals were in power was that they offered to "harmonize" the GST with provincial sales taxes. This put Deputy Prime Minister Sheila Copps in a bind because she had personally promised during the campaign to resign her seat if the GST was not repealed.[43] She actually did resign her seat in 1996 in order to run again in a by-election. She was re-elected and reappointed to cabinet. *Tout est bien qui finit bien.*

Midway through the race, Chrétien and the Liberals appeared to have entered a zone where they could do no wrong. On October 7, Chrétien said while campaigning in British Columbia: "Let me win the election first and then ask me questions about how I would run the government."[44] The sentiments were exactly the same as those of Campbell's remarks of September 23 about campaigns not being the right time to discuss policy, yet they did no harm to the Liberal cause. Campbell was curiously slow to attack Chrétien over his comments, but why were the media so uninterested?

The print media did, in fact, function in this campaign somewhat like the communications department of the Liberal Party. A content analysis of seven major newspapers showed that coverage of Chrétien was far more favourable than that of Campbell. Of stories filed about him, 12 percent were favourable and 24.4 percent unfavourable, whereas for Campbell, only 4.9 percent of stories were favourable and 43.8 percent were unfavourable.[45] Chrétien's favourable-to-unfavourable ratio was 0.49, whereas Campbell's was 0.11. Dividing his ratio by hers, we can conclude that his coverage was 4.5 times as favourable as hers.

Today the world of print media in Canada is not so one-sidedly Liberal as it was in 1993. The founding of the *National Post* and its subsequent merger with the Canwest metropolitan dailies and the *Sun* chain to form Postmedia has levelled the playing field somewhat. But in 1993, newspapers tilted Liberal, even in cities such as Calgary, Edmonton, and Vancouver, where Reform won many seats. The media may not have been the decisive factor in defeating the Conservatives and electing the Liberals in 1993 – after all, Brian Mulroney had had to contend with the same newspapers in his day – but Campbell's political skills were not on the same level as Mulroney's, and the media showed no mercy when she started to stumble.

Gender may have played a role here, too. Campbell's problems in public communication, such as saying too much and straying from the topic, could easily be construed in terms of stereotypes about women's speech. Of Campbell's portrayal in the media, feminist scholar Linda Trimble says:

> To be regarded as prime ministerial, a leader's speech must be "manly" in the sense that it is appropriately confident and commanding, yet controlled and judicious. Campbell's speech mannerisms were often judged to be too revealing, frank, intimate, or loquacious – too "womanly."[46]

If correct, Trimble's evaluation illustrates the cruel irony of politics. Some of the same characteristics that made Campbell seem fresh and attractive to voters, and helped her win the Conservative leadership and restore the party's popularity, may have ultimately contributed to her downfall.

Results

The topline results of the 1993 election are given in Table 4.1.

Only one thing about these results was "normal" in the sense of fitting the expectations that had dominated Canadian politics for the last thirty years: the Liberals got over 40 percent of the vote and won enough seats to form a majority government. Everything else was scrambled. There were now five parties in the House rather

TABLE 4.1
Results of the 1993 general election

Party	Percent vote	Seats
Liberal	41.3	177
PC	16.0	2
NDP	6.9	9
Reform	18.7	52
BQ	13.5	54
Other	3.6	1
Total		295

Source: "Canadian Election Results by Party: 1867–2021," https://www.sfu.ca/~aheard/elections/1867-present.html.

than three. Two new parties, Reform and the Bloc Québécois, had between them won over a third of the seats. The fifty-four seats won by the BQ, a separatist party dedicated to the dismemberment of Canada, made it Her Majesty's Loyal Opposition. The third party, with almost as many seats as the BQ, was the upstart Reform Party of Canada. The NDP, which had been the third party since the 1960s and had recently hoped to move up from that, was reduced to nine seats – not even enough to be a recognized party in the House of Commons. And the Conservative Party, which had alternated with the Liberals in government since 1867, was reduced to a miserable two seats – the biggest loss in Canadian history ever suffered by a governing party in a national election.

Interestingly, voter turnout fell in the 1993 election. Turnout had been 75.3 percent in the two Mulroney elections of 1984 and 1988 but fell to 70.9 percent in 1993.[47] This result seems counterintuitive; one might think that the presence of two new parties with agendas tailored to regional preferences would have increased voter enthusiasm and therefore turnout.

Whatever was happening in voters' minds, turnout in Canadian national elections since 1993 has been consistently lower than in previous decades, when it had usually hovered around 75 percent. After 1993, turnout has never again gone as high as 70 percent.[48] There is general agreement among those who study this subject that declining turnout is the result of the entry of younger people into the pool of voters; older people still vote in traditional proportions, but rising generations are less likely to go to the polls.[49] They can, however, be motivated by leaders who speak their language, as shown by the success of Barack Obama and Justin Trudeau.

Leaving turnout aside, the election of 1993 was a political earthquake and a turning point for Parliament and Canadian politics, at least in the short run. The old issues of deficit spending and the independence of Quebec would be discussed in a different light because the Reform Party and the Bloc Québécois rejected the conventional wisdom of the old parties that deficit spending was necessary to maintain the welfare state and that the separation

TABLE 4.2

Percentage of popular vote by province and territory, 1993

Province/territory	Liberal	BQ	Reform	NDP	PC
British Columbia	28	–	36	16	14
Alberta	25	–	52	4	15
Saskatchewan	32	–	27	27	11
Manitoba	45	–	22	17	12
Ontario	53	–	20	6	18
Quebec	33	49	–	2	14
New Brunswick	56	–	8	5	28
Nova Scotia	52	–	13	· 7	24
Prince Edward Island	60	–	1	7	24
Newfoundland	67	–	1	4	27
Yukon Territory	23	–	13	43	18
Northwest Territories	65	–	8	8	16

Sources: "Past Canadian Federal Election Results," Canada Guide, https://thecanada guide.com/data/federal-elections; "1993 Canadian Federal Election Results by Electoral District," http://esm.ubc.ca/CA93/results.html.

of Quebec was unthinkable. For their part, the old parties could attack Reform and the Bloc as regional and divisive because their support was so obviously tied to particular parts of the country.

Yet to understand the true impact, we have to probe more deeply, down to the regional level. Table 4.2 shows the percentage of popular vote won by each party in each province and territory, while Table 4.3 shows the number of seats won by each party in these jurisdictions. The map on page 2 shows a graphical representation of the data found in Table 4.3.

The first thing to note is that the Liberals were the only truly national party in this election, although their seats were heavily concentrated in Ontario and Atlantic Canada. They won seats in all jurisdictions except Yukon (where there was only one seat, retained by Audrey McLaughlin). They finished first in seven of ten

TABLE 4.3

House of Commons seats by province and territory, 1993

Province/territory	Liberal	BQ	Reform	NDP	PC
British Columbia	6	–	24	2	0
Alberta	4	–	22	0	0
Saskatchewan	5	–	4	5	0
Manitoba	13	–	1	1	0
Ontario	98	–	1	0	0
Quebec*	19	54	–	0	1
New Brunswick	9	–	0	0	1
Nova Scotia	11	–	0	0	0
Prince Edward Island	4	–	0	0	0
Newfoundland	7	–	0	0	0
Yukon Territory	0	–	0	1	0
Northwest Territories	2	–	0	0	0

Sources: "Past Canadian Federal Election Results," Canada Guide, https://thecanadaguide.com/data/federal-elections; "1993 Canadian Federal Election Results by Electoral District," http://esm.ubc.ca/CA93/results.html.

* One Independent also won a seat in Quebec.

provinces as well as in the Northwest Territories. The only jurisdictions where they did not get the greatest number of votes were
British Columbia, Alberta, Quebec, and Yukon. Also, the Liberals
got at least 20 percent of the vote in every province and territory,
showing some degree of support everywhere.

An extreme contrast was furnished by the BQ, which won all of
its fifty-four seats in Quebec, the only province where it ran candidates. Showing its dominance, the party also got 49 percent of
the popular vote in Quebec. Its territorial concentration was even
more pronounced than appears in the table, because all its victories
came in mainly francophone ridings. The one PC and nineteen
Liberal victories in Quebec came in ridings with substantial anglophone and allophone populations – the West Island of Montreal,
Sherbrooke, Gatineau, and a few other enclaves. It was never any
secret: even though the BQ ran candidates in all Quebec ridings, it
was a party of francophones who said they wanted to secede from
Canada.

Reform was almost as territorially concentrated as the BQ,
winning 50 of its 52 seats in the three westernmost provinces
of British Columbia, Alberta, and Saskatchewan. However, Reform
led the popular vote tally only in British Columbia and Alberta.
Although in subsequent elections Reform would also come to
dominate Saskatchewan and Manitoba, it finished behind the
Liberals in these two provinces in 1993. Reform also ran candidates in every other province except Quebec. Although Reformers
won very few seats outside their Western base – 1 in Manitoba and
1 in Ontario – they had the effect of decimating the Progressive
Conservative Party. The Liberals won 98 of 99 seats in Ontario
because the right-of-centre vote was divided between Reform and
the PCs. This was a truly unprecedented result; the Liberals were
giddy with elation as they took seats in rock-ribbed Conservative
ridings they had not won since Confederation. The same thing
happened in Manitoba and Atlantic Canada, where Reform split

the vote in traditional PC strongholds, allowing the Liberals to win 13 of 14 seats in Manitoba and 31 of 32 in Atlantic Canada.

Another important fact about the Reform vote was that it tended to be more rural than urban. Reform did sweep its Calgary mother ship and also won some seats in Vancouver, where the left-of-centre vote was split between the Liberals and the NDP, but it lost four seats to the Liberals in Edmonton and did not win any races at all in Regina, Saskatoon, and Winnipeg. The same trend was visible in Ontario, where Reform performed poorly in the major cities of Toronto, Hamilton, and Ottawa but did better in rural areas, even if not well enough to win seats. However, this urban-rural divide was not much different from that normally seen in Canadian elections. The really novel thing about Reform was that it was dominant or at least competitive almost everywhere in the West, but not a serious factor east of the Manitoba border. This profile, combined with the BQ's dominance in Quebec and the Liberal control of Ontario and Atlantic Canada, marked a degree of regionalization in Canadian politics not seen since 1921, when the Progressives swept the West.

The Conservatives showed some national strength, getting over 10 percent of the popular vote in every province and territory. But that minimal support was not enough to win seats. They did not get above 30 percent of the vote anywhere, and went above 20 percent only in the four Atlantic provinces. Their two victories – Jean Charest in Quebec and Elsie Wayne in New Brunswick – must be attributed to the name recognition and personal popularity of these candidates. Charest had been a highly visible cabinet member, and Elsie Wayne, the former mayor of Saint John, was an institution in that city. In spite of the Liberal landslide elsewhere, she won Saint John for the PCs by 4,000 votes in 1993.

The NDP's support was weaker overall than that of the PCs, but it achieved concentration in a few places, winning a plurality of the popular vote in Yukon, home of leader Audrey McLaughlin, and tying Reform for second place in Saskatchewan. It was in single digits elsewhere, except in British Columbia and Manitoba, where it got over 10 percent. This patchy support enabled the party to elect nine candidates, five of whom were from Saskatchewan, while the others were from British Columbia, Manitoba, and Yukon. Notably, it was shut out of Ontario, even though, or perhaps because, the NDP under the leadership of Bob Rae formed the provincial government there.

What Kind of Election?

One way of summing up these results is found in an oft-cited article by the American political scientist V.O. Key.[50] In Key's terminology, 1993 was a "realigning" election. The term applies to elections in which a combination of new leaders, new parties, and new agenda items produces results that are (1) dramatically different from the preceding election, and (2) persist in subsequent elections. In 1993, there was one entirely new party, the Bloc Québécois, and one almost-new party, Reform, which had been a fringe player in 1988. All parties presented the electorate with new leaders except Reform, and Manning was virtually new because he had played such a small role in 1988. And new agenda items surged to the fore – the separation of Quebec from Canada and the place of the West in Canada.

Francophone voters in Quebec shifted en masse from the Progressive Conservatives to the Bloc Québécois, while many voters in the Western provinces and rural Ontario shifted to Reform, mainly from the Progressive Conservatives. The result was a pattern of representation unlike the one that had prevailed in the House of Commons after the elections of 1984 and 1988: the PCs were now gone from the West and Quebec, replaced by Reform and the BQ, while the Liberals held all but one seat in Ontario. And, as we will see in the next chapter, the new pattern of voter loyalties held firm and even intensified in the "maintaining" elections of 1997 and 2000, until the merger of the old PCs and the new Canadian Alliance (which was essentially Reform under a new name) gave the voters new choices in 2004.

The realignment of 1993 is particularly interesting because Canadian federal politics had gone through another major realignment just nine years earlier. In 1984, it was not only new parties and new issues that stirred the electorate but also new leaders: Brian Mulroney for the Progressive Conservatives and John Turner for the Liberals. Mulroney, as he had promised in his leadership campaign, managed to detach francophone voters in Quebec from their historical allegiance to the Liberals; and indeed francophones in Quebec have never gone back to the Liberals with the same enthusiasm since then. Not being from Quebec, John Turner was ill equipped to meet Mulroney's challenge in that province. The return match between these two leaders in 1988 was a "maintaining" election, similar in result to Mulroney's first victory in 1984 but for some attrition of Conservative seats except in Quebec.

Prior to 1984, the pattern of Canadian federal politics had been generally stable since 1935. The Liberals were the dominant party based on mastery of Quebec, the Conservatives were competitive in English Canada, and the Co-operative Commonwealth Federation (CCF)/NDP had pockets of strength in the West and in Ontario. The only "deviating" election was that of 1958, when support from Quebec premier Maurice Duplessis enabled the PCs led by John Diefenbaker to win francophone votes and seats in Quebec, but this was a one-time victory that Diefenbaker could not replicate on the same scale. He did effectuate a partial realignment by establishing the PCs as the main party of the West, but when the Liberals regained Quebec in 1962, the PCs' new strength in the West was not enough to deliver victory. That's why 1958 was an aberration. It had a realigning legacy as far as the West was concerned, but the change was not broad enough to determine control of the government.

From this perspective, political change bears some resemblances to plate tectonics in geology. Beneath the surface of the earth, plates move slowly but inexorably. Tensions build up until a sudden slip produces an earthquake, sometimes accompanied by a tsunami. The 1984 and 1993 realignments were the earthquake and tsunami of Canadian politics. Two gradual underlying movements had been contained within the previous alignment until they burst out in massive disruption. One was the decline of religious affiliation in Quebec and its replacement by political nationalism, which led francophones to break with the Liberals in 1984 and then move to support a separatist party in 1993. The other movement was the ongoing growth of population and wealth in Western Canada, which exploded in a demand for better treatment in 1993 ("The West Wants In"). These underlying tensions are still there and may someday result in further realignments in Canadian national politics.

A variation on Key's classification of elections has been proposed by Canadian political scientists Lawrence LeDuc and Jon H. Pammett.[51] They emphasize that party allegiance in Canada does not seem as firmly settled as in the United States. It is often said by researchers that only about a third of Canadian voters are firmly committed to a party, while other voters may switch quite frequently, depending upon what is on offer.

LeDuc and Pammett find the term "realignment" to be too long-lasting for Canadian conditions. They prefer to talk about "dynasties" and "interludes." They see Canadian history as consisting of relatively long periods when voters coalesce around a strong prime minister, such as John A. Macdonald, Wilfrid Laurier, William Lyon Mackenzie King, and Pierre Trudeau; Brian Mulroney would have been on this list too, if he had stayed around and won one more election. These "dynasties" are often separated by "interludes," in which party leaders contest with each other until one emerges as a new dynast.

From this perspective, 1993 was the start of a new Liberal dynasty in which Jean Chrétien won three straight majority governments followed by Paul Martin's minority victory in 2004, followed in turn by a Conservative dynasty in which Stephen Harper won three straight victories from 2006 until he was defeated in 2015.

There is merit in both Key's approach and in the one put forward by LeDuc and Pammett. Both are conceptual schemes that can never fit historical events precisely, and it is not worth debating which fits better. Though they may use different vocabulary, both point to the 1993 election as an inflection point, after which politics was never quite the same. That's close enough for government work, as the old saying goes.[52]

Counting Votes

The regional divides that were highlighted in 1993, though real enough, were exaggerated by the first-past-the-post (FPTP) electoral system used in Canada. Under FPTP, (1) the country is divided into territorial jurisdictions called constituencies; (2) each constituency is entitled to elect one and only one Member of Parliament; and (3) the candidate in the riding who gets more votes than any other candidate is elected, that is, the one who would be "first past the post" in a foot race.

A well-established principle of political science, often called Duverger's Law after the French scholar Maurice Duverger, holds that the FPTP electoral system tends to promote a two-party alignment because it helps larger parties win seats at the expense of smaller parties.[53] For example, a party that could draw 10 percent of the vote all over the country would have the support of a lot of people but would win few if any seats. There is one great exception to Duverger's Law, however – regional concentration. As an example of that, take the BQ in 1993. The party won only 13.5 percent of the national vote yet elected fifty-four members because all its votes were in Quebec, mostly in the francophone areas of the province.

A simple way to measure the impact of FPTP in any given election is to divide the percentage of seats won by the percentage of the popular vote received. This creates an index that can range from

TABLE 4.4

Efficiency index, 1993 general election

Party	Percent of popular vote	Percent of seats	Efficiency index
Liberals	41.2	60.0	145.63
BQ	13.5	18.3	135.56
Reform	18.7	17.6	94.12
NDP	6.9	3.1	4.49
PC	16.0	0.67	0.04

zero to almost infinity. Let's call it the "efficiency index," that is, efficiency in converting votes into seats. In a perfectly "fair" electoral system, each party would have an index of 1.0 – that is, each party would win the same percentage of seats as its percentage of the popular vote. Such is the goal of proportional representation, which is never completely achieved but is more or less approximated in countries such as Israel and the Netherlands. But things are different in Canada, and they were especially different in 1993. Table 4.4 shows the efficiency index for Canadian parties in the 1993 general election.

To summarize the results, FPTP rewarded the Liberals for being the largest vote getter by giving them 46 percent more seats than their vote share "deserved." It also rewarded the BQ with a 36 percentage point bonus for extreme territorial concentration. It was more or less "fair" to the Reform Party but grossly "unfair" to the NDP and the PCs. To take the extreme comparison, the Liberal vote was 3,640 times as efficient as the PC vote (145.63/0.04).

In simplest terms, the NDP and the PCs received historically low support in 1993, but the electoral system magnified their deficiencies into stupendously bad results. The Liberals received support across the country, and the electoral system turned their plurality of votes into a comfortable majority of seats. The BQ and Reform did well for themselves by exploiting the tendency of FPTP to reward regional concentration, which of course their party leaders understood. I remember Preston Manning saying that the PCs would be in trouble "because their vote is spread as thin as butter on a slice of bread." His analysis was absolutely correct – for a first-past-the-post system. But if the election had been conducted under any form of proportional representation, the PCs, with 16 percent of the vote, would have won about forty-seven seats, almost as many as Reform's fifty-two. And the NDP would have won about twenty seats, enough to remain a recognized party in the House of Commons.

With two viable new parties in the race, voters faced an unprecedented array of choices in 1993. Where did the new parties find their support? A telephone survey conducted immediately after the election showed that 52 percent of Reform voters and 53 percent of BQ voters had voted for the Mulroney Conservatives in 1988.[54] Both regional parties also attracted much smaller shares from the Liberals and the NDP (and Reform had some supporters returning from its 1988 campaign in the West), as well as new voters and those who had not voted in 1988. But the drawing of votes away from the Progressive Conservatives was the big story of the campaign. To put it another way, the PCs in 1993 retained the vote of only 22 percent of the voters they had attracted in 1988. Historically, there had always been some back-and-forth movement among the PCs, Liberals, and NDP, as there was again this time. But what made the difference was the presence of the two new regionally concentrated parties, which dynamited the Western and Quebec pillars of the Mulroney Conservative grand coalition.

Those familiar with American geography will remember how New Jersey is squeezed between the much larger states of New York and Pennsylvania. Benjamin Franklin is said to have likened New Jersey to "a beer barrel, tapped at both ends," because its commerce tended to flow to Philadelphia on one side and New York City on the other.[55] It's an apt metaphor for what happened to the PCs in 1993, as their supporters flowed for different reasons to two new, widely separated parties. Indeed, the PC barrel was tapped in three places, because a large number of their voters also went over to the Liberals.

How, then, do we explain what happened in 1993? It's an exercise in abductive reasoning, which tries to explain a single outcome through deployment of multiples causes.[56] There is never a single explanation for large-scale historical events, but we have identified several factors that were important in shaping the results of that election:

1 Long-term social and economic trends had contributed to political discontent in Quebec and the West, especially Alberta.
2 Brian Mulroney's grand coalition foundered on its internal contradictions, and Preston Manning and Lucien Bouchard moved in to pick up the pieces in their respective regions. The PCs were thus grievously wounded before the campaign even began, with their hitherto strongest provinces – Alberta and Quebec – obviously on their way out the door.
3 The PCs' new leader did not mesh well with the team inherited from Mulroney, and their campaign turned into a self-destructive shambles.
4 The NDP's new leader was also unable to pull all the elements of her campaign team together. She might have been well suited to a campaign based on identity politics but seemed unable to stand out in an issue landscape dominated by unemployment and deficit spending. Thus the party's campaign, though not as bad as the Conservatives', was far from successful.
5 The Liberals chose the battle-scarred veteran Jean Chrétien as their new leader, and he led them in rebuilding their party and conducting a smoothly running campaign.

6 The first-past-the-post voting system favoured regionally concentrated parties, namely, Reform and the BQ, while hampering
the PCs and NDP, whose support was more dispersed. Thus the
Liberals cruised to a comfortable majority of seats while getting
less than 40 percent of the vote.

Each of these six conditions was not only important but essential
in producing the final result. To see this, conduct a mental experi-
ment that involves nullifying each condition in turn:

1 If religiosity in Quebec had not declined, and if the West had
remained an agricultural backwater, discontent in those regions
would not have been so important. And if the West had not increased its population relative to the rest of the country, its parliamentary seat total would not have been so significant.
2 If Mulroney's grand coalition had not been so weakened before
the election, the Conservatives might have lost in 1993, but they
would not have been reduced to two seats. Reform and the BQ
might have entered Parliament, but not so massively.
3 If the Conservatives had not chosen such an ineffective leader
and run such a bad campaign, they still might have lost control
of the government but would have avoided a rout.
4 If the NDP had chosen a more effective leader, it could probably
have won enough seats to remain a recognized party in the House
of Commons.
5 If the Liberals had chosen a less effective leader, they might not
have won a majority government.
6 Under any form of proportional representation, the Conservatives would have elected a respectable caucus of close to fifty members; Reform, and not the BQ, would have become the official
opposition; the NDP would have remain a recognized party; and
the Liberals would have had to settle for a minority government.

In other words, all six factors worked together to produce the unprecedented result of a Liberal majority government, a BQ official opposition, a large Reform caucus, an unrecognized NDP caucus, and a shattered PC party. By way of comparison, look at two other political factors that surfaced in our discussion of the campaign: declining turnout and creation of the National Party. It wouldn't have made much difference if either or both of these had been different. Even if turnout had been 75 percent rather than 70 percent, there is no reason to think most of those additional votes would have gone in any particular direction and thereby affected the outcome, because none of the leaders in that election had a special appeal to the young people who often don't vote. And the National Party's 1.4 percent share of the popular vote was not big enough to make a difference one way or the other because it was not concentrated anywhere, though the party might have won a couple of seats under forms of proportional representation with a low threshold for entering Parliament.

Note that, other than long-term trends in regionalism, these are all political factors, not demographic, sociological, or economic factors. They are the result of deliberate choices made in politics and government, not of impersonal forces outside anyone's control. The disintegration of the Conservative coalition depended on positions adopted by Mulroney, Manning, and Bouchard. Members of the Conservative, Liberal, and New Democratic Parties chose new leaders, and those leaders made the choices that shaped their campaigns, for better or worse. And the FPTP voting system is a not a fact of nature but a product of legislative choice. It remains in force because thus far Canadians have not been able to agree on which of the many other ways of counting votes might be better.

None of this is to say that demography or sociology or the economy are unimportant to politics; of course, they are very important, because they establish parameters within which political choice takes place. We have already mentioned long-term trends in Quebec and the West. Moreover, the federal deficit and the unemployment rate were both high in 1993. To have any hope of success, a party and its leader had to have policies on at least one of these issues that were credible to a substantial bloc of voters. Manning seized the deficit issue with his Zero in Three proposal. Chrétien captured the constituency for employment measures with his infrastructure program. Campbell tried to triangulate between the two issues but ended up failing to dominate either one. So on the main ideological axis of the campaign, demography and the economy set the stage, while leaders proposed and voters disposed.

Epilogue

Let me close with a personal anecdote. The Canadian Broadcasting Corporation (CBC) invited me to come out to Toronto for election night to represent a Reform perspective. I was no longer working for Reform (I had been fired from my advisory position in August 1993 for giving too much bad advice), but I was still a Reform supporter. The CBC couldn't get anyone representing the BQ to come to Toronto, but there was a hookup with someone from Montreal (I can't remember who it was). And of course there were three panel members with backgrounds in what Preston Manning liked to call the "old line parties."

Late in the evening, when the cameras were off and it was obvious that the PCs were completely vanquished, their representative leaned across me and said to the Liberal, "Can you get ___ a job in the government? He's been driving me crazy looking for work." I thought at the time how ridiculous it was to worry about patronage when your party has just gone down in flames. Years later, after I got to know and respect that person, and I had accumulated more practical experience with political parties, my views softened and I became more political and less moralistic in my judgments.

Prior to the breakup of the Mulroney coalition and the election of 1993, Canadian federal politics had been a somewhat clubby affair, as illustrated by the conversation just related. Many of the leaders and other prominent figures were from Ontario and Quebec. They often knew each other and had been educated at a small number of prep schools and elite universities, such as Queen's, Toronto, McGill, and Laval. Though they put on a great display of partisanship in Question Period and during election campaigns, they actually agreed on political fundamentals, such as the inviolability of the welfare state, the impossibility of doing much about public debt, the need for human rights commissions and affirmative action, the importance of foreign aid and peacekeeping, and the need to pacify Quebec with transfers of money and jurisdiction.

Then came the interlopers, Reform and the Bloc Québécois. Reform challenged all of these elements of ideological consensus, and a great many more, such as multiculturalism and the need for mass immigration. The Bloc accepted most of the earlier consensus but believed that those policies should be implemented in a new country called Québec, not in Canada. Not surprisingly, the old parties saw the two new parties as an existential threat. Canadian politics was being transformed. No longer a gentleman's club enlivened by bouts of electoral cosplay, it was on the way to becoming a war zone.

5

Aftermath

TO UNDERSTAND THE real importance of the 1993 election, as well as the limits of its impact, we have to look at subsequent events, even up to the present day. This is in no sense a complete political history, but rather a selective account of certain threads in the tapestry of Canadian politics that can be traced back to the events of 1993. Looking at subsequent events is essential to deciding whether the 1993 election was more like a pivot or a pirouette.

Reform Goes Mainstream

The immediate aftermath of the 1993 election was relatively calm, though there was endless commentary about the new configuration of political parties and the anomaly of a separatist party being "Her Majesty's Loyal Opposition." The Liberals, however, had a secure majority government, and Prime Minister Jean Chrétien had been a cautious man throughout his long political career, so government proceeded more or less sedately. Of course, the new parties did shake things up a bit. Bloc Québécois leader Lucien Bouchard refused to live in Stornoway, the opposition leader's house, preferring to stay at a Holiday Inn on weeknights and in Montreal on weekends.[1] And the Reform Party made several experiments with procedure in the House of Commons meant to highlight populist democracy.

In the British tradition, a party leader sits in the front row of the Commons, surrounded by his leading ministers or, in the case of an opposition party, the most important critics. Preston Manning chose to sit in the second row, however, projecting an image of being just one member of the caucus. Yet that image was misleading, because both before and after the 1993 election, Manning was very much the controlling figure in the Reform Party. One of the paradoxes of populist parties is that, like all parties, they cannot succeed without strong leadership; otherwise they dissolve into factionalism. The *sine qua non* of populist leadership is to exercise leadership while appearing to carry out the "will of the people."[2]

Another innovation was Manning's appointment of critic teams rather than individual critics, again in order to emphasize the collegial nature of the Reform caucus. This confused the media, however, who were not sure whom to consult for commentary on the issues. Manning also told his caucus members not to heckle, but that hardly stopped the Liberals from showering Reformers with the customary parliamentary abuse.

Perhaps most importantly, Manning led his caucus members in renouncing their parliamentary pensions. This led to a few days of good stories in the media but many more bad stories later on as individual Reformers opted back into the parliamentary pension program. Only three, including Manning himself, stayed out permanently, while most eventually returned.[3] The reality is that unless Members of Parliament are independently wealthy, they need to be earning pension entitlements of some sort because their service disrupts other plans they may have had for funding their retirement. The pension plan at the time was almost absurdly generous and was later trimmed back, but that is different from abolishing it altogether.

None of these or other Reform innovations in House of Commons procedure lasted very long. The customs of parliamentary behaviour have evolved for good reasons, and they are easier to criticize than to change. Reform's procedural changes were amateur ideas developed apart from actual experience in the House, and like most such ideas they were too detached from reality to survive.

It is a bit odd that Manning went down this path because he was a close student of Western Canadian history in the late nineteenth and early twentieth centuries. He certainly knew how the Progressives had limited their influence in the House of Commons when they refused to take up the role of official opposition, even though they had won the second-largest number of seats in the 1921 election. By trying to act as a group of independents, they allowed themselves to be picked off by the cunning Liberal prime minister, William Lyon Mackenzie King. In fact, I remember hearing Preston make this very point in conversation. But for whatever reason, his obvious historical knowledge did not deter him from trying once again to reform the norms of parliamentary behaviour.

Much of the historical francophone vote share of the Liberals in Quebec had gone first to the Mulroney Conservatives and now to the Bloc Québécois, putting the Liberals in a situation that was unprecedented for them in the twentieth century: trying to govern without holding majority support in Quebec. On previous occasions when they had not won a majority of seats in Quebec, the Liberals had landed in opposition in the House of Commons. However, they were now able to dominate Canadian politics even without their historical base in Quebec because the division on the right between Reform and the Progressive Conservatives had given them almost complete ownership of seats in Manitoba, Ontario, and Atlantic Canada.

With Reform and the PCs splitting the Ontario vote about equally, neither party could win seats in that province, leaving the

Liberals laughing all the way to the bank. They won almost every seat in Ontario (about a hundred) in the elections of 1993, 1997, and 2000, and that gave them the base they needed to cruise to a majority in the House of Commons for three consecutive elections. In effect, the Liberals had replaced their historical Quebec base with a new Ontario base. This split on the right enabled the Liberals to survive two crises in 1995 that might otherwise have caused their downfall: a crisis of public finance and a crisis of national unity. The Reform Party would be more involved in the former, the BQ in the latter.

The crisis of public finance involved the federal debt and deficit. (For readers who may not be clear about the distinction between the two, the *deficit* is the current year's excess of spending over revenue, while the *debt* consists of all the government's accumulated obligations to lenders. A deficit becomes part of the debt as money is borrowed to cover it.) The 1993 election took place in the middle of the fiscal year 1993-94, which ran from April 1, 1993, to March 31, 1994. The deficit for that fiscal year was $42 billion and the net debt was $508 billion.[4]

During the election campaign, Chrétien had treated the enormous debt and deficit rather lightly. His solution was to procrastinate, deciding on a deficit target of 3 percent of gross domestic product, which was fashionable in Europe at the time, and to allow three fiscal years to reach that goal.[5] According to the projections in Finance Minister Paul Martin's first budget, that would involve cuts of $17 billion from *projected spending* but almost nothing from *current spending*. In other words, this was not so much a cut in the size of government as a reduction in the rate of governmental growth. The annual deficit would still be about $25 billion in 1996-97, when the target of 3 percent of GDP was supposed to be reached.[6]

Even these not very ambitious goals were soon upset by the course of events, however. Interest rates rose by 400 basis points

(4 percentage points) during 1994, and the Canadian public debt was so large that such an increase meant substantial growth in debt service payments, thereby throwing the government's carefully calculated fiscal framework out of kilter. In round numbers, with a public debt of about $500 billion, each 1 percentage point rise in interest rates meant an extra expense of about $5 billion; an increase of 4 percentage points meant an increase of about $20 billion in interest charges, pushing the annual deficit closer to $50 billion in 1993 dollars, or about $84 billion in 2022 dollars.[7]

Not surprisingly, the bond-rating agency Moody's downgraded Canada's bonds in May 1994, which meant that interest charges would go even higher. In January 1995, the *Wall Street Journal* published a column titled "Bankrupt Canada?" Referencing a recent devaluation of the Mexican peso, the author, John Fund, wrote: "Mexico isn't the only U.S. neighbor flirting with the financial abyss. Turn around and check out Canada, which has now become an honorary member of the Third World in the unmanageability of its debt problem."[8] Fund had become aware of Canada's fiscal crisis in November 1994 when he attended a Fraser Institute conference in Toronto called "Hitting the Wall: Is Canada Bankrupt?"[9] As is often the case, an opinion about Canada coming from an American had more impact in Canada than the same opinion voiced by Canadians.

The *Wall Street Journal* column helped prepare public opinion for what was coming, but Chrétien and Martin had already gotten the message. Starting in the summer, they had forced cabinet ministers to plan how they would deal with serious budget cuts.[10] This was all happening behind the scenes, but occasional hints leaked out. I remember bumping into a former student who was working in Ottawa in fall 1994, and she told me that real cuts were coming. I told her I had heard it all before and didn't believe it, but she swore this time it was real. And she was right.

Paul Martin's budget of February 27, 1995, was truly a landmark. Federal spending was to be cut by $25 billion over three years – not just reductions to anticipated increases, but actual decreases in current spending. Allocations to all departments except Indian and Northern Affairs were reduced; national defence and unemployment insurance were hit particularly hard. Transfers to the provinces were cut by $7 billion, leaving them to bear the brunt of public anger over reduction of services in education, health, and social assistance.

It was strong medicine, indeed. Though the details were different, it was similar in effect to Preston Manning's Zero in Three program; three years later, in 1998, Paul Martin was able to introduce Canada's first balanced budget in thirty years. And the presence of Reform in the House of Commons made it easier for the Liberals to act decisively. When the Progressive Conservatives had been in power under Mulroney and Campbell, opposition had come from the left, from the Liberals and NDP, who constantly attacked the government for being heartless and not spending enough. Now opposition to the government came mainly from the right, from Reform Party MPs, who almost every day in Parliament attacked the Liberal government for not going far enough and fast enough in dealing with the deficit. In this configuration, Chrétien and Martin could impose their draconian cuts and still look somewhat compassionate.

Reform MP and finance critic Herb Grubel told a story in his memoirs that illustrates the dynamic. Grubel, a noted professor of economics at Simon Fraser University before running for Parliament, was invited by Martin to attend a meeting of the International Monetary Fund in Madrid in fall 1994. When they were alone, according to Grubel, Martin

said he needed me and Reform to demand very drastic spending cuts to eliminate the deficit. These demands would allow him and his rather substantial cuts to seem moderate by comparison. They would help him in his fight with members of cabinet and caucus who thought these cuts were not needed, or should be much smaller.[11]

The story is an interesting example of the collaboration that sometimes takes place behind the public Kabuki theatre of parliamentary conflict.

Reform now found itself in the position often occupied by the NDP and the CCF before it, of having signature policies appropriated and implemented by the Liberals as the governing party. For the NDP in the 1970s and 1980s, the thefts had included universal health care and a state-owned oil company (Petro-Canada); for Reform, it was balanced budgets and debt repayment that were purloined. Manning, however, was not satisfied with becoming the "NDP of the right," influencing government policy but never actually governing. He had always wanted a national party with a Western base, a party that could win power, not just exercise influence.

Reform tried again to achieve full national status in the election of 1997, running a full slate of candidates in Quebec. The results were encouraging in some ways, discouraging in others. Reform won sixty seats to displace the Bloc Québécois as the official opposition, but all the gains were in the West, and Reform lost its only seat in Ontario. It was now more than ever typecast as a Western regional party.

The disappointment was heightened by a modest Progressive Conservative recovery under the leadership of Jean Charest, who had replaced Kim Campbell. The PCs won 20 seats, enabling them to regain official party status. Moreover, they won seats in five different provinces, allowing them to brag that they were more representative than the Reform Party, whose seats were all from the four Western provinces. After the PCs' catastrophic result in 1993, Reform had hoped to annihilate them completely and take over their voters, but four years later the PCs showed they were still in the game. Perhaps even more depressing to Reformers was that, with the old Mulroney coalition now split among Reform, the BQ, and the PCs, the Liberals could win 155 of 295 seats with only 38.5 percent of the popular vote – fewer seats than in 1993 but still a comfortable majority. The Liberals were driving in cruise control.

Also, Reform remained at a financial disadvantage compared with the old-line parties. It was able to spend only $4.9 million in the 1997 election, compared with $11.2 million for the Liberals, $10.3 million for the PCs, and $6.0 million for the NDP.[12] The financial struggle was a little more equal than in 1993, but just barely. The PCs still dominated fundraising on the right of the political spectrum. Reform got some financial support from individually owned businesses but only scraps from big business, which found Reform's free-market ideology too radical and the party's populist style alarming.

After disappointing results in the 1997 election, Manning set out to broaden Reform's support by launching the United Alternative campaign. The goal was to build alliances with conservatives in other parties, leading to the launch of a new and larger national conservative party that could compete on more equal terms for votes and dollars. But Jean Charest and the federal Progressive Conservative party absolutely refused to cooperate, even if a few individual members showed some interest. There was more response from members of provincial parties of the right, such as the BC Liberals, the Saskatchewan Party, and especially the Ontario Progressive Conservative party, some of whose most important activists came on board, above all Tom Long, who had been a key adviser to Ontario Conservative premier Mike Harris.

The end result of innumerable discussions, meetings, national conferences, and Reform Party referendums was the creation of a new party, the Canadian Reform Conservative Alliance, usually known simply as the Canadian Alliance. The leadership of the new party was contested by Preston Manning, Tom Long, and Stockwell Day, a Progressive Conservative provincial politician from Alberta who had served in several cabinet portfolios under Premier Ralph Klein. Day's most important post had been provincial treasurer, where he was known for introducing a single-rate provincial income tax, the so-called flat tax. Actually, the new tax wasn't literally flat or single-rate because there was a zero rate on income below a certain level, but the terms were close enough to communicate the essential idea.

Day won the race by a decisive margin. The result seemed unfair to Manning, who after all had founded the Reform Party and conceived the idea of the Canadian Alliance, but no one has ever said that politics is fair. After leading Reform in three national elections and failing to make a breakthrough east of Manitoba, Manning seemed tired and worn out to many Reformers, even though they still revered him as the founder of the movement. Even some who had worked closely with him were looking for new leadership. Stephen Harper threw his support to Tom Long,[13] but more were drawn to Day, who seemed younger, more vigorous, more personable. He had good executive experience and spoke some French, the legacy of a Montreal childhood. I gave his campaign a little money and wrote some favourable columns about him. He looked like a winner for a while, but events would show his limitations as a leader.

Ken Boessenkool, an experienced political operative and observer, once said to me that politicians who have succeeded as finance ministers often have trouble as leaders. The minister of finance is clearly the second most important person in the cabinet after the premier or prime minister, so the department of finance seems like a logical launching pad for winning the top job. But a finance minister really has to do only one major thing a year – prepare the annual budget – for which he is advised by a large staff of bright people, while a leader has to deal day after day with intractable conflicts, somehow keeping the party together in the face of clashing ambitions and beliefs. Often the challenge is not so much to make the perfect decision as to make any decision and move on. Day found the challenge of leadership too much, as did former finance ministers John Turner succeeding Pierre Trudeau and Paul Martin succeeding Jean Chrétien in Canada, Ernie Eves following Mike Harris in Ontario, and Gordon Brown replacing Tony Blair in Great Britain. Of course, all rules about politics have exceptions, and Jean Chrétien, who had been finance minister for a couple of years under Pierre Trudeau, was just such an exception. As prime minister, he seemed to have no trouble making decisions and keeping his desk cleared off.

After winning a by-election in British Columbia, Day entered the House of Commons in summer 2000. He quickly made the flat tax his signature policy and challenged the prime minister to call an early election because "there was a new sheriff in town."[14] The wily Chrétien did call an election for November 27, countering Day's flat-tax policy with an income tax reduction of his own. In the event, the Canadian Alliance improved its vote share by 6 percentage points and increased its seat total from sixty to sixty-six, but with only two in Ontario. Results fell far below expectations, particularly because fundraisers who had come over from the Progressive Conservatives had raised large amounts of money for the Alliance campaign from corporations and wealthy donors.

The Canadian Alliance's electoral performance was not that much better than Reform's, but the party did make huge financial strides. With new support from corporations and wealthy individuals, it was able to spend $9.7 million, compared with $12.5 million for the Liberals, $6.3 million for the NDP, and only $3.9 million for the PCs.[15] The PCs had fallen to fourth in fundraising, compared with 1993, when they had been second behind the Liberals. Reform/ Alliance was already the leading party of the right in terms of votes and seats; now it surged ahead of the Progressive Conservatives in terms of dollars, undercutting the historical claim of that party to represent the business community.

For the time being, however, the Alliance advantage in fund-raising made little difference to the electoral outcome. The Liberals increased their majority in the House of Commons, with 172 out of 301 seats and 40.8 percent of the popular vote. The PCs remained a recognized party, though just barely, with 12 seats. They were now led by Joe Clark, who had returned to federal politics in 1998 after Jean Charest decamped to Quebec to become leader of the prov-incial Liberals. Clark and the Tories reached the 12-seat threshold with the aid of the Liberals, who ran a slack campaign in Calgary Centre, helping Clark get elected there. In the Liberal calculus, having the PCs as a recognized party in the House of Commons could only weaken the ability of the Canadian Alliance to play the role of official opposition.

Day's failure to meet expectations caused significant discontent in the Alliance caucus, many of whom were Manning loyalists who had never been keen to have Day as leader. Though Manning him-self did not leave the Alliance caucus, thirteen others gradually departed to sit in the new Democratic Representative Caucus, where they began merger talks with Joe Clark's Tories. Several senior staffers closely associated with Manning also left their pos-itions. It looked like a slow-motion coup against Day's leadership. This and many other developments caused the Canadian Alliance national council to declare a new leadership race with a voting day of March 20, 2002.

Day decided to run again. Having been leader of the Alliance until recently, he could call on campaigners with fresh experience. His Pentecostal religion made him popular among the more so-cially conservative members of the party and also enabled him to sell new memberships through church connections.

The other main contestant was Manning's erstwhile protégé Stephen Harper, who had been Reform's chief policy officer and was elected to Parliament in 1993, then left before his term was up to become president of the National Citizens Coalition. He never publicly spelled out his reasons for leaving, but he told me privately he didn't think Reform could ever win an election, with or without Manning as leader, because its base was too narrow.

Harper had been out of party politics for seven years and so did not have a set of operatives at hand. He ended up with a team of friends and activists who were long on enthusiasm but short on national campaign experience. As the oldest person in the room, I became his campaign manager. Harper did have the advantage of being well known among the old Reform base, who remembered his prominent role as chief policy officer. We didn't need to sell a lot of new memberships; we won the race through direct mail and telephone contact with the existing membership list, with special emphasis on Alliance members who had earlier been members of Reform.[16]

Harper won a decisive victory, with 55 percent of the votes on the first ballot. He immediately scheduled a meeting with Joe Clark to discuss a merger with the Progressive Conservatives. The leadership campaign slogan had been "Getting It Right," which was meant to imply not only competence compared with some of Stockwell Day's mishaps but also unadulterated conservative ideology. Throughout the campaign, Harper had given the impression that he wanted to preserve the Alliance as a vehicle for robust conservatism, not water it down with Joe Clark's brand of Red Toryism. He couldn't have thought the meeting with Clark would lead anywhere, and it didn't, but now he could say that he had done his best to get a positive response from Clark.

After being rebuffed by Clark, Harper turned his attention to building the Canadian Alliance into a serious competitor to the Liberals in the next election. He quickly moved to reunify the Democratic Representative Caucus with the Canadian Alliance caucus. However, his thoughts turned again to merger with the Tories after a poor Alliance showing in the Perth-Middlesex by-election held on May 12, 2003. In spite of extraordinary efforts, the Alliance candidate finished third, behind the PC and Liberal nominees. Harper's conclusion was that the Alliance could never succeed in Ontario by its own efforts. Opportunity presented itself when Peter MacKay became the new leader of the PCs on May 31 after Joe Clark's resignation. Even though MacKay, in order to get the support of fellow leadership candidate David Orchard, had signed an agreement with Orchard never to merge with the Alliance, Harper correctly judged that this was a political promise that could be broken under the right circumstances.

As soon as MacKay took over the PC leadership, Harper began talking with him, both in public and in private, about a merger. The negotiations were long and difficult; I remember Harper telling me around Thanksgiving 2003 that he didn't think they would succeed. But suddenly they *did* succeed, as Harper gave in to almost all the demands from the PC side. The only thing he insisted on was dropping the word "Progressive" from the new party's name. Other than that, he was flexible. He told me: "I kept saying yes until they ran out of reasons to say no." He thought he could win the leadership of a merged party, and then he could do pretty much what he wanted. Again his judgment proved to be correct, and he became the leader of the new Conservative Party of Canada (CPC) in March 2004.

This leadership race was a bigger and better version of Harper's earlier campaign for the leadership of the Canadian Alliance. His main opponent was political neophyte Belinda Stronach, daughter of auto parts magnate Frank Stronach. Using family money, Stronach was able to assemble a team of talented and experienced campaigners headed by the legendary Tory campaign manager John Laschinger. As part of the merger agreement, the CPC had committed to using the Progressive Conservative leadership selection method of 100 points per constituency regardless of the number of members. Since the party's membership was very weak in Quebec, parts of Atlantic Canada, and downtown Toronto, the rules created about 100 "rotten boroughs" where a candidate could take all or most or the 100 available points by winning over a small number of people. Laschinger's team pursued the rotten-borough strategy effectively, but it was not enough to win; Harper's advantage among the party's mass membership in the West and rural Ontario was simply too great.[17]

After that, the story is well known. With little time to prepare for a national election and without an experienced campaign team, Harper's new Conservative Party lost to Paul Martin's Liberals in June 2004 but managed to reduce them to a minority government. The Liberals won 135 seats, against 99 for the Conservatives, 54 for the BQ, and 19 for the NDP, with 1 Conservative-leaning Independent – 308 seats in all. After the House chose Liberal Peter Milliken as Speaker, the Liberal caucus was reduced to 134. If all Members except the Speaker voted, a majority would require 154 votes out of 307. The Conservatives and the BQ could easily help government legislation pass if they wanted to, but Martin would have preferred to rely on the NDP. Yet the Liberal and NDP vote together was only 153, 1 vote shy of a working majority. All in all, it was not a very stable situation.

It was thus no surprise when Martin's government fell in November 2005; indeed, it had almost fallen in the spring of that year, being saved only when the Speaker broke a tie in favour of the government. (Stronach had added a bit of colour by entering into an affair with Peter MacKay, then defecting to join the Liberal caucus and becoming a minister in Paul Martin's cabinet.) The government fell because the NDP thought it was time for another election. I remember being quite surprised when an NDP strategist made a private call to sound me out about defeating Martin on a confidence vote. I passed the word on to Harper; he was also skeptical at first but spoke with Jack Layton and Gilles Duceppe, and the three leaders managed to get their ducks in a row.

In the ensuing election, the Liberals were defeated and the CPC won its own minority government in January 2006. It won another minority in 2008 and a majority in 2011, before being defeated in 2015 by the Liberals under their new leader, Justin Trudeau.

Stephen Harper was prime minister from February 2006 to November 2015 – almost ten years. In a way, he fulfilled Manning's vision of a national governing party based in the West, except that the CPC was rather different from the Reform Party. The CPC dropped many of the policies that had defined Reform – opposition to official bilingualism and multiculturalism; the direct democracy devices of referendum, initiative, and recall; opposition to corporate subsidies – and adopted others that Reformers would have been uneasy about, such as support for supply management in dairy products.

In 1589, the Huguenot Henry of Navarre is supposed to have said, "Paris vaut bien une messe" (Paris is worth a Mass), when he converted to Catholicism to become King Henry IV of France.[18] Something similar could be said of Harper, the onetime chief policy officer of the Reform Party, who dropped many of the party's policies – ones that he himself had written into the Reform Blue Book – on his path to power.

In political terms, Harper reconstituted two-thirds of the Mulroney coalition, uniting Western Canada with rural and suburban Ontario and Atlantic Canada. But the third pillar, Quebec, always eluded him. He worked on his French until he became quite fluent; he adopted policies designed to be popular in Quebec; he even defined the Québécois as a nation in a House of Commons resolution.[19] But he was never able to win more than twelve seats in Quebec in a general election. It remains a truism of modern Canadian politics that only a leader born in Quebec can win a majority of the seats in that province. Think of Jean Chrétien as well as Pierre and Justin Trudeau for the Liberals, Brian Mulroney for the Progressive Conservatives, Lucien Bouchard and Gilles Duceppe for the Bloc Québécois, and Jack Layton for the NDP. Of course, having been born in Quebec is a necessary but not a sufficient condition. Liberal leader Stéphane Dion, Canadian Alliance leader Stockwell Day, Bloc Québécois leader Gilles Duceppe (in 2011), and NDP leader Tom Mulcair were also born in Quebec but failed to lead their parties to win a majority of seats in the province.

Weakness in Quebec proved to be the CPC's Achilles heel. The party could win government as long as a majority of Quebec seats went to a party other than the Liberals, that is, to the BQ or the NDP, but it lost when the Liberals under Justin Trudeau won a bare majority – 40 of 78 seats – in the province in 2015. Seeing Quebec tilt in a Liberal direction, Harper made desperate attempts to appeal to Quebec nativism, using the term "Old Stock Canadians" (English for *pure laine*), attacking the use of Muslim women's face covering known as the *niqab,* and suggesting a "barbaric cultural practices hotline" for people to report suspicions of female genital mutilation, polygamy, and honour killing. The approach didn't win over Quebec but appears to have boomeranged on the Conservatives in the Ontario suburbs where so many ethnic minorities live.

The moral of the story is that Conservatives can win a national election without major support in Quebec, but only if a party like the BQ or NDP dominates the province and keeps the Liberals from winning too many seats there. For the time being, Mulroney's grand coalition remained "the impossible dream" for Canadian Conservatives, at least without a leader from Quebec.

The Bloc Makes Peace with the System

So much for the fiscal crisis and subsequent history of Reform. We turn now to the crisis of national unity and the part played by the Bloc Québécois.

The Bloc became the official opposition after the 1993 election. Even though Lucien Bouchard and most of his caucus were bilingual, they chose to speak only French in the House of Commons, and all their questions concerned Quebec in one way or another. In the fall of 1994, Bouchard fell ill with necrotizing fasciitis, commonly

After the loss of his left leg, Lucien Bouchard walked with a cane. | Jacques Boissinot, *The Canadian Press*

known as flesh-eating disease, and his left leg had to be amputated on December 1. The amputation, coupled with his recovery from the disease, which could easily have killed him, gave him almost messianic stature in Quebec.

He soon put his new charisma to work in the Quebec referendum on sovereignty scheduled for October 30, 1995. The referendum was the project of Jacques Parizeau, leader of the Parti Québécois (PQ) and premier of Quebec. Parizeau believed there should be a simple yes-or-no referendum question, but polling in the first half of 1995 was not encouraging for such a blunt approach. Parizeau, therefore, had to put some water in his wine to come to an agreement with Bouchard and Mario Dumont, former Liberal youth leader and now head of his own party, the Action Démocratique, to take a more subtle (and ambiguous) approach. The referendum question that came out of their agreement was the following:

Do you agree that Quebec should become sovereign, after having made a formal offer to Canada for a new economic and political partnership, within the scope of the bill respecting the future of Quebec and of the agreement signed on June 12, 1995?

The complicated wording of the question made it a masterpiece of calculated ambiguity, containing references to four different topics: sovereignty, negotiation with Canada, a bill, and an agreement. Many voters would have had trouble articulating just what they were voting for or against. The question was intended to appeal to soft nationalists who might be apprehensive about a clean break with Canada but who thought that threatening to secede might enable Quebec to get a better deal than under the existing Constitution of Canada. The goal was to get a yes vote on something that looked like separation, then move forward from there.

Even with the new wording, however, polling still seemed to show that a yes vote was out of reach. On October 7, therefore, Parizeau stepped down as leader of the yes committee and appointed Bouchard in his place – not an easy step for Parizeau, whose relationship with Bouchard had always been tense. Reaction in Quebec to Bouchard's appointment was electric. As he toured the province for three weeks, hobbling on his cane and using all his oratorical power, support rose for the yes side. In the end, the result was, from a federalist point of view, frighteningly close, 49.4 percent yes to 50.6 percent no. Canada had really dodged a bullet. We learned later that, in spite of the softer, indeed deliberately confusing, wording of the question, Parizeau had prepared detailed plans for issuing a unilateral declaration of independence if the yes side had triumphed – an eventuality for which Canada was not prepared.[20]

Parizeau resigned as premier and PQ leader the day after the referendum loss, and Bouchard went to Quebec City at the end of 1995 to take over those jobs, serving as premier until 2001. After the referendum, and without Bouchard's charismatic leadership, the Bloc remained nominally separatist but in reality morphed into a regional party representing the interests of Quebec within Canada. Bouchard's successor, Gilles Duceppe, was not as charismatic as Bouchard – no one could have been – but he was politically astute. Under his leadership, the Bloc had its ups and downs but continued to win the largest number of seats in Quebec in the next five elections – 1997, 2000, 2004, 2006, and 2008. With separation off the table, it feasted on local Quebec issues such as biker gangs and the sponsorship scandal, often known as "Adscam," in which it was revealed that federal grants in Quebec had secretly been funnelled to the federal Liberal Party.

Starting with the election of 2004, when the Canadian Alliance and the Progressive Conservatives merged and no longer competed against each other, the BQ took enough seats in Quebec to prevent both the Liberals and the Conservatives from winning a majority government. Everything changed, however, in 2011, when the NDP under Jack Layton's leadership caught fire and won 103 seats, including an astonishing 59 in Quebec. The Bloc was reduced to 4 seats and Duceppe resigned as leader. He returned in 2015 to lead the Bloc to 10 seats, not much to cheer about but enough to keep the party alive. Then he resigned again, and the Bloc appeared to be on its last legs. Surprisingly, though, it bounced back under a new leader to win 32 seats in 2019 and 32 in 2021, not a majority of ridings in Quebec but enough to deny the Liberals a majority government. The BQ was back to playing the spoiler.

The NDP's success in 2011 surprised everyone, including themselves. It was a long and difficult road for the party from 1993, when it had been reduced to 9 seats and lost official status, to 2011, when it won 103 seats and became the official opposition. After its historic defeat in 1993, the NDP replaced leader Audrey McLaughlin with Alexa McDonough. Cynics joked that it was an economy measure because they could keep on using the initials "A.M." on all the party stationery (admittedly not a very funny joke). McDonough had been NDP leader in Nova Scotia and led the party to 21 seats in the 1997 general election, including several in Atlantic Canada, where it did much better than ever before. The party fell back to 13 seats in 2000, however, and the McDonough era was over.

The next leader, former Toronto city council member Jack Layton, took the NDP to unprecedented heights after an entire decade of patient work. Under his leadership, the party moderated its rhetoric and modernized its approach to politics, relying more on professional pollsters and advertisers.[21] The NDP won 21 seats in 2004, 29 in 2006, and 37 in 2008, as it increased its vote share in each election, drawing particularly on former Liberal voters.[22] The big payoff came in 2011, when the NDP won 103 seats and became the official opposition. In addition to the former Liberal voters that it continued to attract across the country, the party surged ahead in Quebec, going from 1 seat and 12 percent of the vote in 2008 to 59 seats and 43 percent of the vote in 2011. By far the largest proportion of its new voters were francophones who had formerly voted for the Bloc Québécois.[23]

How to explain the NDP's quantum leap between 2008 and 2011? The party had the same leader, Jack Layton, and the same policies, more or less, as before. The Conservatives and the Bloc also had the same leaders, Stephen Harper and Gilles Duceppe, and the same policies, more or less. To be sure, it was important that the Liberals had a new leader, Michael Ignatieff, who failed to connect with Quebecers in spite of his excellent Parisian French and his undoubted reputation as a world-famous author and filmmaker. But the previous Liberal leader, Stéphane Dion, had also failed to win a majority of seats in Quebec in spite of being a native of the province and having an impressive academic reputation.

Observers cited Layton's affable personality, and indeed he was likable. I knew him slightly during my time in Ottawa, and I couldn't help liking him even though our political views were diametrically opposed. He would easily have passed the folkloric test, "Would you like to have a beer with this guy?" But he had always been affable, so why would his personality suddenly have so much greater effect in 2011? Observers also often cited his command of French, which, though not elegant, was effective in a street-wise sort of way (Layton had been born and had grown up in Montreal). But his French had always been what it was, so why would it make such a difference in 2011?

What was new this time was that Layton had recently been diagnosed with prostate cancer. He was treated and recovered to the extent that he could campaign, but he had to walk with the aid of a cane. Shades of Lucien Bouchard campaigning in the 1995 separation referendum after having lost a leg! The gritty story of recovery from a near-death medical experience seemed to touch something in the Quebec psyche. Polling data show that Quebec voters saw Layton as by far the most attractive leader in 2011, especially because he "cared about ordinary people" and "was inspirational."[24]

Because the NDP ran candidates all over the country, its success had a different effect upon Canadian politics from that of the BQ. The NDP did well in 2011 in numerous suburban ridings in Ontario, taking votes away mainly from the Liberals, which enabled the Conservatives to win many of these seats and thus earn a majority government. The Conservative popular vote was only 2 percentage points higher in 2011 than in 2008, but the blows delivered by the NDP to the Liberals helped the Conservatives win a lot more seats. One of the great themes of Liberal campaign rhetoric over the years had been that a vote for the NDP would help elect a Conservative government, and that warning came true in 2011.

Unfortunately for the party, Layton died of cancer shortly after the election, and his successors could never match his appeal. The NDP fell to forty-four seats in the 2015 election under the leadership of former provincial Liberal cabinet minister Tom Mulcair, even though he was from Quebec and fluently bilingual. With Jagmeet Singh as leader, they fell even further to twenty-four seats in 2019 and twenty-five in 2021, with only one in Quebec each time. Singh speaks excellent French, but he is not from Quebec, and his appearance as a bearded and turban-wearing Sikh would seem foreign to some voters in a province where Bill 21 has prohibited public employees from wearing religious symbols.[25] He tried to counteract that in 2019 by appearing in a French-language video without his turban, but it was obviously not enough.[26]

After all the years of *Sturm und Drang*, the NDP was back where it had started, a third party far from exercising power but having influence because its votes were keeping the Liberal minority government in office. Indeed, after the elections of 2019 and 2021, all the parties were back more or less to the positions they had occupied in 2004. The Liberals had a minority government, the Conservatives were the official opposition, the Bloc was in third place after winning enough seats to ensure that the Liberals could not form a majority government, and the NDP was in fourth place. Did Yogi Berra really say, "It's like déjà vu all over again"? At any rate, this outcome leads directly to the topic of the next chapter, equilibrium and disequilibrium in the Canadian party system.

No matter how many and severe the shocks it may suffer – and the shocks in 1984 and 1993 were indeed severe – the Canadian political system tends to revert to the status quo ante. Observers will have their own opinion as to whether the return to equilibrium is good or bad, but it does seem to be a persistent tendency. Yet the disruptions to equilibrium are equally important, and the essence of Canadian politics lies in the balance of the two.

6

The Punctuated Equilibrium
of Canadian Politics

Equilibrium is a central concept in rational-choice analysis, as it is in economics generally. It refers to an outcome at which rational actors will arrive by pursuing their own self-interest. Market prices are the classic example. Motivated by self-interest, buyers and sellers arrive at a price where supply and demand curves intersect. The price is stable as long as underlying conditions remain the same, but a supply constraint, innovative technology, or a change in tastes leading to an increase or decrease in demand can shift the curves, leading to a new equilibrium price.

In the abstract models of economics and game theory, equilibrium is a precise mathematical solution, but the term is also often applied in a less rigorous sense to describe the stability of institutions and political configurations. Thus, when political scientists speak of a "party system," they mean that certain political parties, supported by relatively stable coalitions and competing within a fixed legal framework, divide up the vote in more or less predictable ways. For example, a kind of equilibrium prevailed in Canadian national politics from 1867 through 1917. Although smaller parties existed, only the Conservatives and Liberals could win enough seats to become government and opposition. It was a classic "two-party system."

Things have never been that simple since then. Starting with the election of 1921, there have always been at least three, and sometimes four or five, parties that could win enough seats to assume importance in the House of Commons. Added to the Liberals and Conservatives were the Progressives starting in 1921, the Co-operative Commonwealth Federation (CCF) and Social Credit in 1935, Reform and the Bloc Québécois in 1993, and the Greens in 2011. These parties were born from an overlapping mix of crisis events, regional strains, and ideologies that could not be accommodated within the original two-party system.

To describe Canadian politics over the century since 1921, let us borrow the concept of "punctuated equilibrium" from evolutionary biology.[1] It provides a colourful metaphor to describe the ebb and flow of Canadian politics. Coined by Niles Eldredge and Stephen Jay Gould in 1972, the notion of punctuated equilibrium hypothesizes that periods of stability are separated by unpredictable times of rapid change brought on by shifts in climate, landscape, or even extraterrestrial events such as a meteorite strike. Biologically, the result is the generation of new species, or the spread of existing species that had previously lived in the shadow of others; think of the rise of mammals after a giant meteor strike 65 million years ago led to the extinction of the dinosaurs.[2]

Applying the metaphor to politics, periods of disruption are marked by the rise of new parties (the mammals) to challenge the old parties (the dinosaurs). But in Canadian politics, the dinosaurs have survived by borrowing from the mammals, containing them in limited feeding grounds, and absorbing or merging with them. Seen in this perspective, the election of 1993 was not a unique disruption of Canadian politics but one in a series of disruptions by which Canadian politics is periodically adapted to changing conditions.

The 1993 election was a spectacular deviation from what had gone before, but it also gradually led to a new equilibrium, different from but with many similarities to the old one. The previous chapter showed how things gradually went back to earlier norms. The 1993 election was pivotal in the sense of introducing highly visible changes into Parliament and politics generally – new parties, new leaders, and new agendas. It confirmed that Quebec would no longer be the playground of the Liberal Party. But over a longer time frame, the pivot came to resemble a 360-degree pirouette, as Reform merged back into something very much like the traditional Progressive Conservative (PC) Party, and the Bloc Québécois lost its separatist edge. Now let's think more analytically about what happened to these two new parties. The rational-choice theory of electoral competition will help provide an explanation.

Reform and Regionalism

The Reform Party, moved by its desire to win more seats and form a government, morphed into the Canadian Alliance. The Alliance in turn, driven by the same imperative, merged with the Progressive Conservatives to form the Conservative Party of Canada (CPC). Some PCs, such as former leader Joe Clark and his Nova Scotia colleague Scott Brison, who had once resigned his Commons seat so Clark could run there in a by-election, left the new party, but most stayed. And as time went by, the CPC came to look more and more like the old Progressive Conservatives, as it jettisoned the more controversial policies inherited from Reform.

Yet as long as Stephen Harper was leader of the CPC, it had a definite Western flavour. Many of the most important ministers in the cabinet were from the West and had entered politics through Reform or the Alliance. In addition to Harper himself, think of Stockwell Day, Jason Kenney, Jim Prentice, Rona Ambrose, Monte Solberg, Chuck Strahl, and James Moore, all of whom became recognizable national figures. But Harper retired after losing the 2015 election, and none of his other leading Western cabinet ministers are still in federal politics.

In an interesting echo of Brian Mulroney's retirement, none of Harper's Western cabinet heavyweights, or those from other parts of Canada such as Peter MacKay and John Baird, chose to seek the leadership when Harper retired. Those who decided to run were secondary figures in cabinet; indeed, the eventual winner, Saskatchewan MP Andrew Scheer, had never even been in cabinet, though he had been Speaker of the House. Serving for years under dominant personalities such as Mulroney and Harper may cause the highest-profile ministers to start making other plans. Unwilling to risk a suicidal challenge of the leader, and not knowing when he will step down, they start dreaming of becoming a provincial premier or making the "big bucks" as a rainmaker for a law firm or a bank director.

Andrew Scheer was forced out after failing to win enough seats to form a government in 2019. Even though the CPC under his leadership got more votes than the Liberals, it didn't elect as many MPs. Many of the Conservative votes were "wasted" because the party ran up larger than necessary majorities in Alberta and Saskatchewan. The CPC conducted a leadership race in 2020 without any Western candidates. The winner was Erin O'Toole, an MP from Ontario who had briefly been minister of veterans affairs in 2015 and who had also run for the leadership in 2015. He won the majority of points (each constituency had 100 points to be distributed among the candidates according to their percentage of the vote) in Quebec with a targeted Quebec platform, reviving the strategy that Harper had used in the general election of 2006 to make a mini-breakthrough (ten seats) in the province.[3]

O'Toole then went on to woo Quebec with a special platform in the 2021 general election.[4] The results were disappointing, however, as he was facing two Québécois leaders, Justin Trudeau for the Liberals and Yves-François Blanchet for the Bloc Québécois. Against that home field advantage, the Conservatives were unable to improve their seat total in Quebec, even with a quasi-endorsement from Quebec premier François Legault.[5]

Having failed to improve upon Andrew Scheer's showing, O'Toole was then forced out by a vote of the Conservative caucus, and a new leadership race was ordained, with the vote to be held in September 2022. At the time of writing, the two leading candidates in a numerous field appear to be Pierre Poilievre and Jean Charest.

Poilievre grew up in Calgary but has represented an Ottawa riding in Parliament since 2004. He served as a minister in the latter years of Stephen Harper's government. Though now living in Ontario, he is the favourite of the Western populist wing of the party and takes positions reminiscent of the old Reform Party. Yet he is fluently bilingual, which may help him broaden his support.

Jean Charest was discussed earlier in this book. Though he is now stressing his conservative economic and fiscal record as Liberal premier of Quebec, he appeals more to the old Progressive Conservative element of the party.

If Charest wins, it will be an ironically striking "back to the future" moment. It will be somewhat like the Progressive Conservatives' embrace of Brian Mulroney in 1983, based on his promise of being able to deliver Quebec. Charest was elected along with Mulroney in 1984, was a loyal member of his caucus and cabinet, became leader of the Progressive Conservatives, refused to consider a merger with Reform and the Canadian Alliance, and left for Quebec provincial politics after a merger took place. Unlike Mulroney, Charest may not be able to "deliver Quebec" (he could not even win his own seat the last time he tried), but he will project a more moderate image than Poilievre, which may be useful in large parts of Ontario and the Atlantic provinces.

No matter who the new leader turns out to be, the additional seats required to propel the Conservatives to victory probably have to be mainly the suburban Ontario seats that Harper won in 2011 but lost in 2015, and that have not been recaptured by the Conservatives since then. Everyone assumes that Western voters will fall into line and support the CPC no matter who the leader is. To put it in terms of political history, it's like Conservative politics before Preston Manning founded the Reform Party. The West is considered a reliable part of the Conservative voting coalition but is not expected to call the shots. As far as Reform and the West are concerned, politics has come full circle.

Are the seeds of a new populist movement already starting to sprout in the West? The Reform Party now belongs to history, but Preston Manning foresaw the possibility of a revival. He said in the party's early days: "The Western populist parties have a more natural life cycle than the traditional parties. They live, they die, the seeds go into the ground and then they come up again, perhaps in a different form."[6] The day after the Liberals won the 2019 election, posters went up in Edmonton advertising the existence of the new Wexit party – "Wexit" being shorthand for "West Exit," rhyming with Brexit, the movement championing Great Britain's exit from the European Union. No one took Wexit seriously at first because it was extremely small and its leader was a political unknown. Then the first leader stepped down in favour of Jay Hill, a former Conservative MP and House Leader under Stephen Harper.

Not long after winning the leadership, Hill persuaded Wexit members to rebrand themselves as the Maverick Party,[7] a move designed to broaden the party's appeal. The Maverick Party made a dismal showing in the 2021 election, however, getting only 33,000 votes and not coming close to winning any seats. It was upstaged by Maxime Bernier's People's Party of Canada (PPC), which, though not winning any seats, increased its share of the national popular vote from 1.6 percent in 2019 to 5.1 percent in 2021.

Although it has espoused some Western issues, such as opposition to carbon taxes, the PPC is not a Western populist party. It is a national party founded and led by a Quebec libertarian who was once a Conservative MP and cabinet minister and came very close to winning that party's leadership in 2017. Its surprisingly good showing in 2021 seemed due not to the regionalism that animated Reform but to new issues such as climate change and COVID-19, on which the larger parties were not offering much choice to voters. One should not predict success for the PPC; indeed, most new parties fail. But it would also be foolish to ignore the party, just as those who tried to ignore Reform were mistaken. Like the Greens at the other end of the left-right spectrum, it offers a voice to voters who don't see their views reflected in the more established parties.

Reform and the Median Voter

The fate of Reform is an interesting story in its own right, but it also has an explanation from rational-choice coalition theory, one branch of which is known as the median voter theorem. This theorem explains how participants can go about assembling a winning coalition in any decision-making system based on voting.

First, a few key concepts. The *median* is the midpoint of a distribution. Consider a distribution consisting of the three observations 10, 20, and 60. Twenty is the median because there is one observation below it (10) and one above it (60). But 20 is not the *mean* of the distribution. The mean is 30 because $(10 + 20 + 60)/3 = 30$.

The median voter theorem was one of the earliest results in the field of rational choice. It applies to all decision-making bodies ranging from small committees such as the nine-member Supreme Court of Canada to large bodies such as the millions of Canadian voters in an election. The theorem says that if there is only one dimension of difference among the voting members, and if each member has an ideal point somewhere along that dimension, and if the body proceeds by majority rule, then any winning coalition must contain the median voter.[8] This means that the median voter is *pivotal* and can dictate the outcome.

An illustration will make this easier to understand. The Chief and Council of a small First Nation are meeting to decide how much to budget for snow removal on their roads next winter. Each member has an ideal point:

A	$50,000
B	$60,000
C (Chief)	$80,000
D	$85,000
E	$90,000

There are two possible rational winning coalitions: A, B, and C; and C, D, and E. Coalitions such A, B, and D or B, D, and E are possible but irrational because in the first one D would have to accept $60,000, and in the second one B would have to accept $85,000. The general principle is that rational voters choose an outcome as close as possible to their own ideal point and don't jump over intervening possibilities.

In this scenario, the Chief (C) gets his way not because he is the Chief; he has only one vote, just like each of the Councillors. He gets his way because he is the median voter and is pivotal in any rational coalition. He can say to A and B, "Vote with me for my ideal point and you will get an outcome of $80,000, which is more than you would ideally like to spend but is less than you will have to spend if you make a coalition with D or E." Similarly, he can say to D and E, "Vote with me and you will get an outcome of $80,000, which is less than you would ideally like to spend but more than you will spend if you make a coalition with A or B." Thus the Chief as median voter dictates the outcome because no rational (connected) majority coalition is possible without him. In the language of rational choice, the median voter is *pivotal* to any winning coalition.

The application of the median voter theorem to electoral politics was first drawn by the American economist Anthony Downs.[9] Like all rational-choice models, it requires making several assumptions that, while not strictly true, do apply much of the time to many situations. One has to assume that there is only one dimension of difference that matters to voters (say, left-right) and that all who choose to vote have an ideal point somewhere along that dimension. Assume further that only two political parties compete for support, and that their major method of attracting voters is to adopt positions along the left-right spectrum. Finally, assume that voters are rational so they vote for the party located closest to their ideal point. If all these assumptions are met, then both parties will position themselves near the median voter – that is, they will adopt ideologically similar centrist positions while competing for votes in other ways such as emotional appeals or attacks upon the personality of the opposing leader.

This is not a bad description of political party competition for much of the history of the Anglo-American democracies. Labour and Conservatives in Britain, Democrats and Republicans in the United States, Liberals and Conservatives in Canada, Liberals and Labor in Australia, and Labour and National in New Zealand have often held quite similar ideological positions beneath the rhetoric of electoral competition. When I was a graduate student in the 1960s, hugging the centre was said to be essential to winning elections. Test cases were the candidacies for US president of Republican Barry Goldwater in 1964 and Democrat George McGovern in 1972. Goldwater was said to be too far to the right, McGovern too far to the left, which is why both men lost in landslides.

The simple diagrams of Figure 6.1 illustrate the point.

If party B positions itself away from the median voter (M) by moving further to the right, there will be many voters to the right of M who are now closer to party A than to party B, assuming that A sticks close to M. Specifically, all the voters to the left of the midpoint of the line segment MB are now closer to A than to B. By the logic of rational choice, party A gets the support of all voters to its left plus those to the left of the midpoint of MB, and now wins in a

FIGURE 6.1
The median voter theorem

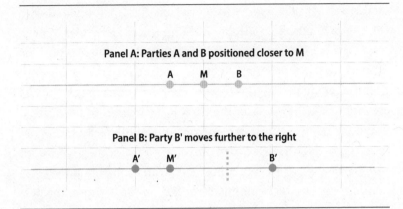

landslide. The same thing would be true in reverse if party A positioned itself away from M by moving to the left. Party B would now hold its support on the right and pick up the support of voters to the right of the midpoint of the line segment MA. Thus ran the rational-choice explanations of how Lyndon Johnson crushed Barry Goldwater in 1964 and Richard Nixon crushed George McGovern in 1972.

The logic of the median voter theorem as applied to electoral competition is compelling yet strangely disconcerting. Democracy is supposed to be about choice, yet the theorem teaches us that there really is no choice, for the winning position is always that of the pivotal median voter. It is the politics of Tweedledum and Tweedledee, heads I win, tails you lose. Politics is like Macbeth's tragic view of life, that it is a "tale told by an idiot, full of sound and fury, signifying nothing."[10]

Fortunately, Downs's simple model is not the whole story. One of his key simplifying assumptions is that only two parties compete for votes. This applies reasonably well (though not perfectly)

FIGURE 6.2

The rational-choice model of third-party invasion

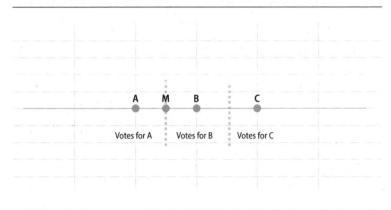

to the United States, but is off the mark for the other Anglo-American democracies. In particular, Canada has had three or more viable parties for a whole century, ever since 1921, when the Progressives crashed the gates of Parliament to join the Liberals and Conservatives.

So let's relax the assumption that only two parties compete for votes but let's keep the rest of Downs's model. If we start with a two-party system in which both parties are positioned close to the ideal point of the median voter, how could a new party invade, when the midpoint is already so crowded? Invasion from the centre is indeed difficult, but invasion from the margin, from either the left or the right, is often a viable strategy.[11] Consider Figure 6.2.

Traditional parties A and B are positioned close together near the median of the voter distribution, one party (A) claiming to be slightly more left-wing, the other (B) claiming to be slightly more right-wing. That makes voters further away from the median open to predation by new parties. Suppose party C positions itself to the right of B, as shown in Figure 6.2. It is now closer to all the voters whose ideal point is to the right of C, plus those voters in the right half of the line segment BC. If new party C gets its positioning right, it can hope to undermine party B by capturing a large chunk of B's electoral support.

This is essentially the game that Reform played against the Progressive Conservatives starting with the 1988 election (and that Maxime Bernier and the PPC would like to play against the contemporary Conservatives). It wasn't quite that simple, because Preston Manning had envisioned a party based in the West that could draw support from all parts of the left-right spectrum. He said as much in his famous hockey analogy, in which he speculated that Reform, like a hockey team, had to have a right wing, a centre, and a left wing.[12] But the people who were attracted to Reform turned out to be overwhelmingly conservative in orientation, and they wanted a party that was more purely conservative in ideology than the Progressive Conservatives.

The electoral strategy for Reform was fairly obvious. I remember a planning meeting that took place in 1991 or 1992, when I was working for Reform. We were trying to designate targeted ridings where we could hope to win the seat by deploying extra effort, when Monte Solberg suddenly broke in. "It's easy," he said. "We just pitch to ridings where the PCs have been strong, and we take away their vote." And that's what happened. Monte hadn't studied rational choice, but he had the shrewd judgment of a natural politician. In the election of 1993, Reform positioned itself like party C in Figure 6.2, cutting off the Progressive Conservatives from much of their historical base. As a result, the PCs were decimated, losing all their seats in the West and Ontario. Reform took most of those Western seats but only one in Ontario, where Reform's Western image conferred no advantage.

Having captured the West and weakened the PCs, the next logical step for Reform was to win erstwhile Progressive Conservative seats in Ontario and the Atlantic provinces, thus becoming able to compete for government. But that would have required a move to the centre, towards the median voter where the PCs used to position themselves, and Reform found it impossible to make that move, not least because it was typecast by the other parties as racist, extreme, and un-Canadian.

Reform thus found itself stuck on the further right of the spectrum. It had *displaced* the PCs, reducing them to insignificance, but it had not *replaced* them. Rather, the Liberals had been able to take advantage of the ruined PCs, winning almost all their traditional constituencies in Ontario and Atlantic Canada. Thus, in the new equilibrium the Liberals were able to cruise to three majority government in the elections of 1993, 1997, and 2000, because Reform, while strong enough to win in the West, proved unable to take over the remaining PC votes in Ontario and the East. Manning tried to complete his invasion from the margin with his Canadian Alliance project, but that proved insufficient. It was not until Stephen Harper pulled off a merger with the remaining Progressive Conservatives, and the Liberals had weakened themselves by factional infighting between the supporters of Jean Chrétien and of Paul Martin, that the new Conservative Party became competitive with the Liberals and could win government.

The story is deeply ironic. Reform could *ruin* the PCs but could not win an election on its own. In order to win, Reform had to *become* something like the 1980s version of the PCs, assuming that party's position near the median voter. As Peter MacKay, Stephen Harper's merger partner, told the first Conservative Party of Canada policy convention in 2005, the new party needed to be "a moderate, mainstream national alternative."[13] In the language of rational choice, that meant positioned near the median voter. Most of the old policies that had made Reform distinctive were expunged from the policy book at that convention.

Is invasion from the margin also a Shakespearean "tale told by an idiot, full of sound and fury, signifying nothing"? Quite the contrary. The invading party brings with it new policies that may become acceptable in the mainstream of politics. In destroying the old equilibrium and creating a new one, it may help shift the position of the median voter, at least for a period of time. In Reform's case, it ran interference for the ideas of balancing the budget and paying down debt, which the Mulroney PCs had espoused and accomplished to a degree, but far from completely. In 1995, the Liberal government picked up Reform's emphasis on fiscal responsibility, balanced the budget in three years, and thereafter started to pay down debt. It was the beginning of a decade of fiscal responsibility that lasted until 2008, when the so-called Great Recession caused the Harper government to loosen the purse strings temporarily. But Harper returned to balanced budgets by the end of his majority government in 2015.[14] Reform may have failed to win an election, but it succeeded in another sense by helping to create a new policy consensus among the major parties and voters at large that deficits and debt were to be avoided if possible.

That consensus lasted until 2015, when Justin Trudeau ran and was elected on a policy of deliberately incurring deficits. Trudeau's break with the past seemed not too great at first, but then the COVID-19 pandemic intervened in 2020. The federal debt is projected to rise above $1 trillion in 2022,[15] about 45 percent of the expected gross domestic product.[16] Our federal debt will be in the same range as a percentage of GDP in the mid-1990s when the Chrétien government decided to move towards a balanced budget, with the aim of stopping the growth of the debt and thereby preventing a run on the Canadian dollar.[17]

The Bloc Québécois: Finding a Niche in the System

The case of the Bloc Québécois was different in important ways from that of Reform. Its political raison d'être was to gather together all who wanted to bring about the independence of Quebec, regardless of ideology. Conservatives, liberals, social democrats – all were

FIGURE 6.3
Two-dimensional politics

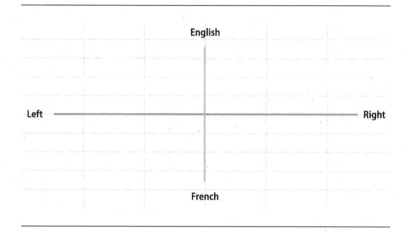

welcome. It was strangely like Preston Manning's early strategy of trying to assemble Westerners under the Reform banner, regardless of what party they had supported before. But unlike Reform, the BQ never aspired to win a national election and form the government of Canada.

Figure 6.3 illustrates the BQ's strategy in the graphic terms of two-dimensional politics. The BQ introduced a new dimension of difference that cut across the standard left-right dimension. Actually, "emphasize" would be a better word than "introduce," because the dimension of conflict over the status of Quebec is always part of Canadian politics. At one end is the extreme position of the independence of Quebec; at the other end is the view that Quebec is a province *comme les autres,* with no special rights or status. In between are several intermediate positions with names like "sovereignty-association," "distinct society," and "special status." Generally speaking, federal politicians try to play down this dimension because it threatens the existence of Canada as a sovereign state. But it has come to prominence from time to time in Canadian history, as in the conflicts over conscription during the two world wars.

It rose to prominence again in the 1960s, perhaps because the decline of the Catholic Church in Quebec allowed national identity to take the place of religious identity. Whatever the deep causes of the separatist movement may have been, federal politicians tried to contain it. For Pierre Trudeau, the Canadian Charter of Rights and Freedoms, with its guarantees of bilingualism, would beat back separatism. Brian Mulroney's talismans were the Meech Lake Accord, and then the Charlottetown Accord. After much bickering, the three major federal parties – Liberals, Progressive Conservatives, and NDP – coalesced around these three projects of institutional reform as they were put on the table, but they never satisfied francophone opinion in Quebec.[18]

Separatism entered the mainstream in Quebec under René Lévesque, who led the Parti Québécois to victory in the provincial election of 1976. Fifteen years later, Lucien Bouchard broke up the fragile consensus of the federal parties over institutional reform and made separatism an option for Quebec voters in federal elections. His rhetorical genius led francophone voters in Quebec to think not about left-centre-right but about the desire to make Quebec a sovereign nation. It has been said that the key to politics is not to tell people *what to think*, but *what to think about*. Bouchard personified that adage precisely, by making Quebec voters think about sovereignty above all else. His new dimension of difference destroyed the equilibrium formed by the old parties around constitutional reform and enabled the formation of new political coalitions.

With his charismatic campaign in the sovereignty referendum of 1995, Bouchard came close to achieving his goal, though perhaps not as close as one might think. Even if there had been a majority yes vote, and even if Premier Jacques Parizeau had immediately issued a unilateral declaration of independence (UDI), as we now know he planned to do,[19] many obstacles remained. The referendum question had been made deliberately ambiguous to let some voters think they were demanding a new offer from the rest of Canada, not immediate independence. How would they have reacted to a UDI?

That's just the beginning of the unanswered questions. What about the Inuit and First Nations of Quebec, who had forcefully expressed their opposition to the separation of Quebec from Canada?[20] What about the anglophone and allophone minorities concentrated on the West Island of Montreal? Would Canada have recognized the UDI, or would it have branded it a violation of constitutional law? Parizeau was counting on support from France,[21] but would other countries, above all the United States, have recognized Quebec as an independent state, particularly if Canada asked them not to?

These questions remain counterfactual, so we are not pressed to give answers. But they illustrate the immense institutional inertia confronting the separatist project. It is not surprising that after 1995 the BQ has contented itself with being the voice of francophone Quebec and not pressing the issue of sovereignty. Parliament also made separatism more difficult by passing the Clarity Act, giving federal politicians some control over the wording of future referendum questions and over the interpretation of referendum results.[22] Like Reform, though in a different way, the BQ was beaten by "the system." Reform wanted to win national elections and so had to merge with the PCs to get closer to the median voter. The BQ didn't care about winning national elections, but it wanted to build majority support in Quebec for separation. When it didn't succeed in that project, it became a regional party within the Canadian party system, relentlessly advocating on behalf of its home province.

Was it all wasted effort? Many Quebec voters would surely say no, for by deploying the separatist threat, Quebec has gained a long list of privileges enjoyed by no other province. Let's begin with Robert Bourassa's famous "five conditions" for approving the Constitution Act, 1982. These are the demands that led to the Meech Lake negotiations: recognition of Quebec as a distinct society, a Quebec veto over constitutional change, a provincial role in the appointment of Supreme Court justices from Quebec, greater control over immigration, and limits on the federal spending power. To be sure, Quebec did not get these all guaranteed in one tidy document, but it has received much of the substance of these demands through a combination of federal legislation, Parliamentary resolutions, and administrative action.

1 *Distinct society.* These particular words have not been enshrined in law, but Quebec received something similar through a House of Commons resolution introduced by Prime Minister Stephen Harper on November 22, 2006: "That this House recognize that the Québécois form a nation within a united Canada." BQ Leader Gilles Duceppe had planned to introduce a motion recognizing Quebecers as a nation, but Harper outmanoeuvred him by adding the words "within a united Canada."[23] In the end, all parties, even the BQ, supported Harper's motion.

2 *Veto over constitutional change.* Late in the 1995 referendum campaign, Prime Minister Chrétien promised to give Quebec a veto over future constitutional changes. The way he fulfilled this promise was through the so-called five-region veto, which conferred veto power not only on Quebec but also on Ontario, British Columbia, the three Prairie provinces taken together (in which Alberta has an internal veto because it contains more than half the population of the Prairies), and the four Atlantic provinces taken together (in which Prince Edward Island has no actual weight because of its small population). The five-region veto was not itself a constitutional amendment but a piece of ordinary legislation prohibiting the federal cabinet from introducing a

constitutional amendment unless it had the prior support of all five veto-wielding regions.[24]

3 *Supreme Court justices.* Under a new appointment process announced by Prime Minister Trudeau in 2016, new justices will be recommended by an advisory panel. In 2019, when one of the three seats from Quebec became open, the members of the advisory committee were drawn almost entirely from Quebec.[25]

4 *Immigration.* Under a 1991 agreement with the federal government, Quebec received the right to select immigrants to that province,[26] a right that it has used to increase the number of francophone immigrants or those open to "francisation" (having some background in French language and culture or willing to learn). Although the agreement does not give Quebec the right to keep immigrants in the province if they wish to move elsewhere, it does give the province a first crack at choosing immigrants who might be willing to live in a province where French is the majority language.

5 *Federal spending power.* In the past, the federal government has used its spending power to create welfare programs within provincial jurisdiction, such as health care, social assistance, and aid to university students. The spending power has not been limited by legislation or court decision, but if Ottawa does undertake major new spending programs, Quebec will be allowed to opt out with compensation for its own equivalent program.

Obviously, the BQ is not solely responsible for all these gains for Quebec; indeed, the government of Canada started making concessions almost as soon as the separatist movement arose in the 1960s. But the BQ is ever ready to speak out on any issue where Quebec's interests might be engaged. None of Quebec's privileges is carved in constitutional stone, but it would be a foolhardy politician who would be tempted to try to take them away.

The foregoing list is only a small sample of the ways in which Quebec's political leaders have achieved their political objectives. To mention only a few more: Quebec has its own representative in Canada's delegation to UNESCO as well as its own delegation to L'Organisation internationale de la Francophonie. The budget of Radio-Canada takes up a disproportional amount of the budget of the Canadian Broadcasting Corporation. The equalization formula is carefully engineered so that Quebec receives about 65 percent of the transfers. One of the ways in which this result is achieved is by not including renewable resources (think Hydro-Quebec) in the definition of fiscal capacity.[27]

The BQ did not bring about these features of Canadian public policy, some of which existed long before the party was founded. But imagine trying to change them – the Bloc would be at the forefront of protest in the House of Commons. The provincial government of Quebec is undoubtedly more important in the political process, but the Bloc has a preferred position in Parliament. It is thus an important part of the network of institutions by which the position of Quebec in Canada is protected.

Equilibrium and Innovation

The moral of the story here is the punctuated equilibrium of the Canadian political system. It was seriously challenged by the emergence of new parties in 1993; for a while, it seemed that everything was up for grabs. And yet, almost three decades later, it may seem that nothing much has changed. Driven by a desire to win elections, the Reform Party merged with the Progressive Conservatives. While Stephen Harper was Conservative leader and prime minister, the new party had a Western flavour; but now, with Harper and other leading Westerners back in private life, the CPC looks pretty much like a reincarnation of the Progressive Conservative Party without the word "Progressive" in its title. Indeed, former leader Erin O'Toole openly pursued a median voter strategy in the 2021 election;

and, if Jean Charest is chosen to be the next leader of the party, he will undoubtedly go the same way, but with more credibility because of his Progressive Conservative background.

Unlike Reform, the Bloc Québécois is still around under its original name, but it has survived only by coming to terms with the continued existence of Canada It was a close call, but separatism was beaten back in 1995. Now the BQ is for all practical purposes a regional party, protecting the interests of Quebec within Confederation. Admittedly, it did have a near-death experience in 2011, when it was almost wiped out by the NDP. If not for Jack Layton's death, the NDP might have finished the job, but now the BQ is back. With 32 seats in 2019 and 2021, it has real power in a Parliament of minorities. The governing Liberals needed the support of just one other party to pass legislation, and that party could be the CPC, the NDP, or the BQ. If the Bloc has to put up with being part of Canada, that's a pretty good position to hold.

And just to make the irony complete, politics going forward will have to reckon with the trillion-dollar-plus debt caused by trying to deal with the COVID-19 pandemic. Shades of 1995! In Canadian politics, parties and policy agendas keep coming back, while issues also tend to recur. How many times has Canada dealt with major crises of national unity between Quebec and the rest of the country? Think of Louis Riel's insurrection in 1885, the conscription crises of 1917 and 1944, and the separation crisis that ran from the 1960s to the 1990s. Now the federal public debt, having been tamed after the Second World War and again in the 1990s, seems poised to make another comeback. Maybe Kim Campbell was right to quote Ecclesiastes: "There is nothing new under the sun."

What happened in 1993 and afterwards is just the most recent illustration of the tendency of the Canadian political system to equilibrate. The Liberals appeared to be in huge trouble in the First World War, when the party split and many Liberal MPs supported Robert Borden's Union government. But the Liberals came back to power in 1921, and with them the Progressives, who won more seats than the Conservatives and could have been the official opposition if they had wanted to accept that role. They were conflicted about party government and chose to stay aloof, however, enabling Liberal prime minister Mackenzie King to outmanoeuvre them and gradually bring many of them back into the Liberal fold. Thus the Conservatives re-emerged as the main alternative to the Liberals.

The election of 1935 brought Social Credit and the CCF into Parliament, but nothing fundamental changed in terms of who got to run the government. The Liberals governed from 1935 to 1984, except for the 1957–63 interregnum of John Diefenbaker's Progressive Conservatives and the 1979–80 blip of Joe Clark's minority PC government. It still remains true that since Confederation no party has formed a government except the Liberals and Conservatives, though other parties have occasionally formed the official opposition (the BQ in 1993–97, Reform-Alliance in 1997–2004, and the NDP in 2011–15).

Yet this is not to say that long-term change never happens. An earlier chapter discussed how dominance in Quebec was the basis of Liberal power for almost a century, from 1896 through the election of 1980; but that dominance disappeared in 1984, when Brian Mulroney's Progressive Conservatives swept the province, and has never really returned. The PCs won a big majority of seats in Quebec in 1984 and 1988, then the BQ more or less inherited their francophone vote and won a majority of Quebec seats in 1993, 1997, 2000, 2004, and 2008. When the BQ collapsed in 2011, the NDP won a majority of seats in the province. The Liberals came back in 2015 with a narrow majority of seats, 40 out of 78, but lost that distinction in 2019, when the Bloc made a surprising comeback. The Liberals still won a plurality of seats, 35 of 78, but the BQ was right behind with 32. Then that outcome was repeated in 2021.

To summarize, in the twelve federal elections from 1984 to the present, the Liberals have won a majority of seats in Quebec only once (and that was narrow) and a plurality of seats only twice. At different times Quebec has been dominated by the PCs, the BQ, the NDP, and the Liberals (barely). The Liberals are again competitive in Quebec but far from dominant, even with a francophone leader from Quebec.

The election of 1993 did not create this change in Quebec, but it set the seal on it. If Quebec had gone back to the Liberals in 1993, when Liberal leader Jean Chrétien was a francophone from the province, the Mulroney years could have been seen as an aberration, but 1993 showed that a deeper change had taken place. The Liberals can still win federal elections by amassing support in Ontario and in Atlantic Canada, with some seats in Quebec, but they haven't been able to rely on a solid Quebec base as they did in elections from 1896 through 1980. So fundamental changes in political alignments do take place, even if it may take decades to establish their longevity.

That said, it is also still true that the Canadian political system exhibits tremendous inertia in the face of challenges from new parties. Yet this inertia does not mean that new parties are unimportant. Canadian political life would be uncreative without them. What could be more boring than the spectacle of two big parties engaged in sumo wrestling near the median voter, hardly differing in policy but campaigning on themes of party loyalty, leader's image, and scary stories about the other? Politics would be little more than name-calling. It is the new parties that have brought in new ideas.

The Progressive threat forced Ottawa to pay attention to Western issues, such as the transfer of Western public lands and natural resources from federal to provincial control. The CCF pioneered major themes of the welfare state, such as universal medical insurance. Social Credit in 1935 spoke for Albertans who were being crushed by mortgages; having been the last province to be settled, Alberta carried an enormous debt load when the Depression struck in 1929. Reform drew attention to Western grievances while putting the issues of the public debt and deficit on the table. The Bloc Québécois spoke for the nationalistic dreams of francophone Quebecers. The Greens have pushed the other parties to pay attention to environmental issues that they might have preferred to ignore. The People's Party of Canada is now criticizing the conventional wisdom on climate change and COVID-19 vaccinations.

Of course, the ironic outcome is that the new parties have never managed to govern at the national level.[28] Either they are too far from the median voter or the new dimensions they raise do not have the power to totally supersede the left-right dimension. But they often exercise influence by forcing the old parties to take account of their issues. As Liberals liked to say about the CCF, they were "Liberals in a hurry."

That's how the Canadian system evolves. New parties arise, full of passion and enthusiasm. The existing parties heap scorn upon them at first, but sometimes they eventually realize that they will have to deal with the issues highlighted by the new parties. In effect, the newcomers change the position of the median voter, and the whole system shifts to a new equilibrium. Thus new and smaller parties are as essential to Canadian politics as the historical governing parties. By bringing about innovations that would be lacking if the Liberals and Conservatives were left undisturbed to court the median voter, they help the "system" adapt to the ceaseless changes of Canadian society.

Appendix 1
List of Key Players

Aberhart, William (1878–1943): Founder of the Alberta Social Credit League and premier of Alberta, 1935–43. Former high school principal and fundamentalist radio preacher.

Allaire, Jean (1930–): Influential provincial Liberal in Quebec. Broke with the party in 1994 to form the Action Démocratique du Québec, a nationalist but not separatist party. Retired as leader after a few months because of poor health, in favour of Mario Dumont.

Ambrose, Rona (1969–): Conservative MP from Edmonton, 2004–17, and member of Stephen Harper's cabinet. Interim leader of the Conservative Party of Canada, 2015–17.

Anderson, Rick: Manager of the Reform Party's campaign in the 1993 federal election. Had previously been a Liberal organizer and strategist but became alienated from the party after the election of Jean Chrétien as leader. Pursued a career as a political consultant after 1993 while also remaining connected with conservative political parties and causes.

Baird, John (1969–): Conservative MP from Ottawa, 2006–15, and member of Stephen Harper's cabinet. Had previously been a Progressive Conservative MLA and member of the Ontario cabinet for Mike Harris and Ernie Eves.

Balagus, Michael: Senior NDP staffer who briefly became controversial in the 1993 campaign for hiring an American firm to get a job done. Later became chief of staff to NDP leaders in Manitoba and Ontario.

Barrett, Dave (1930–2018): NDP premier of British Columbia, 1972–75. Elected to Parliament in 1988; lost the subsequent NDP leadership race to Audrey McLaughlin.

Beck, John: Member of the Toronto taxi-owning family who became a Reform Party candidate in 1993 but embarrassed the party with racist statements and was dropped as a candidate.

Bernier, Maxime (1963–): Conservative MP for Beauce, Quebec, 2006–19, and member of Stephen Harper's cabinet. Son of Gilles Bernier, who had held the same seat for the Progressive Conservatives. Founded the People's Party of Canada in 2018 after losing a close leadership race to Andrew Scheer. The party has not elected anyone to Parliament.

Blair, Tony (1953–): Labour prime minister of the United Kingdom, 1997–2007.

Blanchet, Yves-François (1965–): Bloc Québécois leader and MP since 2019. Previously a PQ MNA and cabinet minister in Quebec.

Boessenkool, Ken: Policy adviser to Stephen Harper in the early years of Harper's leadership. Longtime activist in conservative political parties who has also worked for leaders such as Stockwell Day and Christy Clark, the Liberal premier of British Columbia.

Borden, Robert (1854–1937): Conservative prime minister of Canada, 1911–20.

Bouchard, Lucien (1938–): Founder and first leader of the Bloc Québécois. Studied at Laval and practised law in Chicoutimi. Known as a nationalist and separatist in politics, but was nevertheless appointed by his friend Brian Mulroney to be ambassador to France in 1985. Ran for the House of Commons in 1988 as a Progressive Conservative and then entered Mulroney's cabinet. Initially supported the Meech Lake Accord but left the cabinet when he thought the accord was being watered down. Formed the Bloc Québécois in 1990, then became leader of the opposition in 1993. Led the yes side in the 1995 sovereignty referendum, then left Ottawa to enter Quebec politics in 1996. Premier of Quebec until he retired in 2001.

Bourassa, Robert (1933–96): Liberal premier of Quebec, 1970–76 and 1985–94. Involved in many struggles over the constitution; particularly remembered as a proponent of the "distinct society" slogan.

Brison, Scott (1967–): Progressive Conservative MP from Nova Scotia, 1997–2003. Went over to the Liberals after the PC merger with the Canadian Alliance. Subsequently served as a Liberal MP and cabinet minister until retirement from politics in 2019.

Broadbent, Ed (1936–): Leader of the NDP, 1975–89. Professor of political science before getting elected to the House of Commons in 1968 from the Ontario seat of Whitby. Pushed out as NDP leader after the 1988 election because the party did not do as well as hoped, even though the NDP won an all-time high number of seats in that election.

Brown, Gordon (1951–): Labour prime minister of the United Kingdom, 2007–10. Previously Chancellor of the Exchequer under Tony Blair, 1999–2007.

Byfield, Ted (1928–2021): Founder of the *Alberta Report* and allied magazines, which espoused a merger of conservative Christianity and politics that had powerful influence in Western Canada. Gave important support to the foundation and growth of the Reform Party.

Campbell, Kim (1947–): Prime minister of Canada, 1993. Born, raised, and studied in British Columbia. Entered Parliament in 1988 and served in several cabinet portfolios under Brian

Mulroney. After defeating Jean Charest in a contest for leader of the Progressive Conservative Party, became the first and still only female prime minister of Canada but served only about four months as she led her party to a catastrophic defeat in the 1993 election.

Carville, James (1944–): American political consultant credited with inventing the war room for rapid response in the 1992 election while working for Bill Clinton.

Charest, Jean (1958–): Elected to Parliament in 1984, and served as minister under Brian Mulroney. Unsuccessfully ran for the Progressive Conservative leadership against Kim Campbell in 1993. Leader of the Progressive Conservative Party, 1995–98. Leader of the Liberal Party of Quebec, 1998–2011, and premier of Quebec, 2003–11. Candidate for leadership of the Conservative Party of Canada, 2022.

Chrétien, Jean (1934–): Prime minister of Canada, 1993–2003. Born to a poor family in Shawinigan Falls, QC. Studied law at Laval. Elected to the House of Commons in 1963 and served in several cabinet posts under Pierre Trudeau. Lost the 1984 Liberal leadership race to John Turner, but was chosen Liberal leader in 1990, then led the Liberals to three majority governments in the elections of 1993, 1997, and 2000. In spite of his electoral success, was pushed out by Paul Martin, who organized party members against him; resigned in 2003.

Clark, Joe (1939–): Prime minister of Canada, 1979–80. Born in High River, AB. Studied political science at the University of Alberta. After serving as an assistant to Alberta premier Peter Lougheed, was elected to Parliament in 1972. Became Progressive Conservative leader in 1976 and won a minority government against Pierre Trudeau's Liberals in 1979. Miscalculating his support in the House of Commons and in the nation, was defeated in a non-confidence vote in late 1979 and lost the subsequent election. Defeated by Brian Mulroney for the PC leadership in 1983, but served in Mulroney's cabinet and played a key role in the negotiations leading to the Charlottetown Accord.

Clinton, Bill (1946–): Democrat president of the United States, 1993–2001. Previously governor of Arkansas.

Copps, Sheila (1952–): Elected to Parliament in 1984 after serving as a Liberal MLA in Ontario. Finished third in the 1990 Liberal leadership race behind Jean Chrétien and Paul Martin. Served as deputy prime minister, 1993–96. Ran unsuccessfully for the Liberal leadership against Paul Martin in 2004, then returned to her original field of work in the media, becoming a columnist and broadcast host.

Day, Stockwell (1950–): Leader of the Canadian Alliance, 2000–02. Had been a minister in the Progressive Conservative cabinet of Ralph Klein in Alberta, and went on to become a minister in Stephen Harper's Conservative federal cabinet until retiring in 2011 to become a political consultant.

Diefenbaker, John (1895–1979): Prime minister of Canada, 1957–63. Lawyer. Elected as the MP for Prince Albert in 1940 and became Progressive Conservative leader in 1956. Under his leadership, the party won a minority government in 1957, gained a huge majority in 1958, and another minority government in 1962. His government was defeated on a motion of non-confidence in 1963, after his cabinet split over the issue of nuclear weapons. Lost the leadership in 1967 but remained in Parliament until his death in 1979.

Dion, Stéphane (1955–): Leader of the Liberal Party of Canada, 2006–08. Had been a minister in the Liberal governments of Jean Chrétien and Paul Martin. Prior to entering politics, had been a professor of political science, well known as an outspoken critic of separatism.

Duceppe, Gilles (1947–): Leader of the Bloc Québécois, 1996, 1997–2011, and 2015. Leader of the opposition, 1993–97. After a career as a union organizer, was elected to the House of Commons in 1990 as an Independent and quickly joined the new Bloc Québécois. Served in Parliament until 2011 and 2015–19. Replaced Lucien Bouchard as leader of the BQ after Michel Gauthier proved ineffective.

Dumont, Mario (1950–): President of the Liberal Youth Commission but left the party in 1994, together with Jean Allaire, to found the Action Démocratique du Québec, a nationalist but not separatist party. Leader of the ADQ, 1994–99, becoming leader of the opposition in the Quebec National Assembly in 1997. Left politics in 1999 to become a radio and TV broadcaster.

Duplessis, Maurice (1890–1959): Founder of the Union Nationale and premier of Quebec, 1936–39 and 1944–59.

Eggleton, Art (1943–): Liberal MP, 1993–2004. Subsequently appointed to the Senate. Mayor of Toronto for eleven years before entering federal politics. Held several cabinet portfolios under Jean Chrétien.

Eves, Ernie (1946–): Finance minister in the Progressive Conservative government of Mike Harris in Ontario and leader of the party, 2002–04.

Fairbairn, Joyce (1939–2022): Liberal Senator from Alberta, 1984–2013. Had been a Liberal staffer before the appointment. Served in the cabinet as Senate majority leader after the 1993 election.

Finley, Doug (1946–2013): Conservative campaign manager, 2005–08. Born in England but raised in Scotland, worked at a senior level in business before devoting himself to political organization. Director of operations and deputy campaign manager for the Canadian Alliance and Conservative parties before becoming campaign manager. Appointed to the Senate in 2009.

Gregg, Allan (1949–): Progressive Conservative pollster in the 1993 campaign. Founded the polling company Decima Research and was the pollster for the Progressive Conservatives in the 1984 and 1988 campaigns. Sold Decima after the PCs' 1993 debacle and later founded the consulting firm Strategic Counsel.

Grubel, Herb (1934–): Reform Party MP and finance critic, 1993–97. Professor (now emeritus) of economics at Simon Fraser University.

Harper, Elijah (1949–2013): Helped defeat the Meech Lake Accord in 1990 by filibustering against ratification in the Manitoba Legislature. Chief of the Red Sucker First Nation, then a member of the Manitoba legislature, 1981–92, and cabinet minister in the NDP government, 1986–88. Liberal MP for one term, 1993–97.

Harper, Stephen (1959–): Chief architect of the 2003 merger between the Canadian Alliance and Progressive Conservative Party. Prime minister of Canada, 2006–15. Born and raised in Toronto. Moved to Calgary, where he studied economics and became chief policy officer of the Reform Party and the main draftsman of the party's Blue Book. Elected to Parliament in 1993 as a Reformer but left in 1997 because of unhappiness with Preston Manning's leadership. Re-entered politics in 2001 and became leader of the Canadian Alliance. Re-elected to Parliament in a by-election in 2002.

Harris, Mike (1945–): Leader of the Progressive Conservative Party of Ontario, 1990–2002, and premier of Ontario, 1995–2002.

Hill, Jay (1952–): Reform/Canadian Alliance/Conservative MP from British Columbia, 1993–2010. House Leader for the Conservative government of Stephen Harper, 2008–10. Leader of the Wexit/Maverick Party, 2020–.

Hnatyshyn, Ray (1934–2002): Governor General of Canada, 1990–95. Progressive Conservative MP, 1974–88, and member of Brian Mulroney's cabinet, 1985–88.

Hošek, Chaviva (1946–): Coauthor of the 1993 Liberal Red Book. Prominent feminist. Served one term as a Liberal MPP and cabinet minister in Ontario, 1987–90. Important policy adviser for the federal Liberals, 1990–2001, and helped write their 1997 and 2000 election platforms.

Hurtig, Mel (1932–2016): Founder and leader of the National Party, which contested the 1993 election but did not elect anyone. Had been an Edmonton bookseller, then a publisher. One of the founders of the Committee for an Independent Canada (1973) and the Council of Canadians (1985), also a candidate for the federal Liberals in 1972.

Ignatieff, Michael (1947–): Leader of the Liberal Party of Canada, 2008–11; led the party to its worst result ever in the 2011 election. Well-known author and filmmaker. Taught at Harvard, among several universities. Rector of the Central European University in Budapest, 2016–11.

Kenney, Jason (1968–): Reform/Canadian Alliance/Conservative MP from Calgary, 1997–2016; held several portfolios in Stephen Harper's cabinet. Co-founder of the United Conservative Party in Alberta in 2017, and UCP premier of Alberta, 2019–.

King, William Lyon Mackenzie (1874–1950): Liberal prime minister of Canada, 1921–1926, 1926–30, and 1935–48.

Lalonde, Marc (1929–): Liberal MP from Quebec, 1972–84. Held several cabinet portfolios under Pierre Trudeau and (briefly) under John Turner. Minister responsible for introducing the National Energy Program in 1980 and conducting the subsequent negotiations with Alberta.

Laschinger, John: Executive director of the Progressive Conservative Party in the 1970s. Introduced direct mail fundraising to Canadian politics. Served as campaign manager for many, mainly conservative, candidates, though he has also worked for NDP candidates in Toronto. Author of two books on campaigning in Canada.

Laurier, Wilfrid (1841–1919): Liberal prime minister of Canada, 1896–1911.

Layton, Jack (1950–2011): Leader of the NDP, 2003–11, and leader of the opposition, 2011. Came from a political family; his father was an MP from Quebec and a member of Brian Mulroney's cabinet. Studied at McGill University, then York University, where he earned a PhD in political science. Active in Toronto city politics until winning the NDP leadership in 2003. Led the NDP to its best result ever in 2011 but died of cancer shortly thereafter.

Legault, François (1957–): Cofounder and leader of the Coalition Avenir du Québec from 2011, and premier of Quebec since 2018. Parti Québécois MNA, 1998–2009, and cabinet minister, but renounced separatism when founding the CAQ.

Lévesque, René (1922–87): Founder and first leader of the Parti Québécois, 1968. PQ premier of Quebec, 1976–85. Liberal MNA, 1960–70, and member of the cabinet in Quebec. Former journalist.

Loewen, Bill (1930–): Prominent Winnipeg businessman and philanthropist. Bankrolled the National Party in 1933, and subsequently fell out with leader Mel Hurtig.

Long, Tom (1958–): Unsuccessful candidate for leadership of the Canadian Alliance in 1990. Lawyer. Chaired successful Ontario Progressive Conservative election campaigns for Mike Harris in 1995 and 1999, and had held many other positions in the federal and provincial Progressive Conservative parties. Runs an executive search firm.

Lougheed, Peter (1928–2012): Progressive Conservative premier of Alberta, 1971–85. Proponent of adding s. 33, the "notwithstanding" clause, to the Charter of Rights and Freedoms.

Macdonald, John A. (1815–91): Conservative prime minister of Canada, 1867–73 and 1878–91.

MacKay, Peter (1965–): Last leader of the Progressive Conservative Party of Canada, 2003, and cofounder, along with Stephen Harper, of the Conservative Party of Canada, 2003. MP from

Nova Scotia, 1997–2015, and held several portfolios in Harper's government, 2006–15.

Manning, Ernest (1908–96): Social Credit premier of Alberta, 1943–68. Late in his career, tried to arrange a merger or coalition with the Progressive Conservatives, both federally and in Alberta, but his attempts did not succeed.

Manning, Preston (1942–): Son of Alberta premier Ernest Manning. Educated at the University of Alberta and worked as a consultant with his father. Led the formation of the Reform Party of Canada in 1987. In 1993, the Reform Party surprised observers by winning fifty-two seats in the House of Commons. Became leader of the opposition after the 1997 election. Led the movement to broaden Reform's base by transforming it into the Canadian Alliance but lost the leadership of the new party to Stockwell Day in 2000, and retired from the House of Commons in 2002.

Martin, Paul, Jr. (1938–): Liberal prime minister of Canada, 2003–06, and finance minister, 1993–2002. Son of Paul Martin, Sr., a leading Liberal politician. Studied law at the University of Toronto. Worked for Power Corporation and became CEO of Canada Steamship Lines. Liberal MP for the Montreal riding of LaSalle–Emard, 1988–2008. Lost a leadership race to Jean Chrétien in 1990. After serving successfully as finance minister, managed to oust Chrétien by organizing party members against him and became prime minister in late 2003. Was reduced to a minority government in 2004 and defeated by Stephen Harper in 2006.

Massé, Marcel (1940–): Liberal MP and cabinet minister, 1993–99. After a career in the civil service in which he rose to be clerk of the Privy Council, was recruited in 1993 to run for the Liberals in Hull, QC. Not to be confused with Marcel Masse, who was a Union Nationale and Progressive Conservative politician.

Mazankowski, Don (1935–2020): Deputy prime minister, 1986–93, and minister of finance in Brian Mulroney's cabinet. Progressive Conservative MP from Alberta, 1968–93.

McDonough, Alexa (1944–2022): Leader of the NDP, 1995–2003. Previously leader of the Nova Scotia NDP, 1980–94, becoming the first woman to lead a recognized political party at any level in Canada.

McLaughlin, Audrey (1936–): Leader of the NDP, 1989–95, and the first woman to lead a major federal party in Canada. Born and raised in Ontario. Former social worker. Entered the House of Commons after winning a by-election in Yukon in 1987. Became NDP leader in 1989. Announced her resignation after leading her party to a poor showing in the 1993 election and did not run for re-election in 1997.

Milliken, Peter (1946–): Liberal MP from Kingston, ON, 1988–2011, and speaker of the House of Commons, 2001–11.

Moore, James (1976–): Canadian Alliance/Conservative MP from British Columbia, 2000–15. Held several portfolios in Stephen Harper's government. Subsequently became Chancellor of the University of Northern British Columbia.

Mulcair, Tom (1954–): Leader of the NDP, 2012–17. Had previously been a minister in the Liberal government of Jean Charest in Quebec.

Mulroney, Brian (1939–): Progressive Conservative prime minister of Canada, 1984–93. Born in Baie-Comeau, QC, the son of an Irish-Canadian electrician; grew up fluently bilingual. Studied at St. Francis-Xavier and Laval Universities. Practised law in Montreal. Was defeated by Joe Clark in 1976 for the leadership of the Progressive Conservative Party, but then defeated Clark for the same position in 1983. Under his leadership, the Progressive Conservatives won a landslide victory in 1984 and another majority government in 1988. He announced his retirement from politics in 1993.

Newman, Peter C. (1929–): Prominent journalist and author of many books on Canadian politics and history.

Orchard, David (1950–): Candidate for the leadership of the Progressive Conservative Party of Canada in 1998 and 2003. Known for his anti-Americanism. Moved to the Liberals after the 2003 merger between the Progressive Conservatives and the Canadian Alliance.

O'Toole, Erin (1973–): Conservative leader, 2020–21, and MP for Durham, ON, 2012–. Forced out of his leadership position after the Conservatives under his leadership won more votes but fewer seats than the Liberals. Former officer in the Canadian Forces and a corporate lawyer.

Pantazopoulos, Dimitri: Researcher for the Reform Party of Canada in the run-up to the 1993 election. Subsequently specialized as a pollster, working for many conservative candidates and parties. Now the principal at Maple Leaf Strategies.

Parizeau, Jacques (1930–2015): Parti Québécois premier of Quebec, 1994–96. Retired from politics after the yes side lost the 1995 referendum

Pearson, Lester (1897–1972): Liberal prime minister of Canada, 1963–68. After a career in the foreign service, was appointed Secretary of State for External Affairs in 1948 and won a seat in the House of Commons shortly afterwards. Became Liberal leader in 1958. Announced his retirement at the end of 1967. Though his term as prime minister was relatively brief, and he always led a minority government, he was responsible for several important policy innovations, such as the Canada Pension Plan.

Poilievre, Pierre (1979–): Conservative MP from Ottawa, 2004–. Member of Stephen Harper's cabinet. Candidate for leadership of the Conservative Party, 2022. Born in Calgary, adopted by francophone parents.

Prentice, Jim (1956–2016): Conservative MP from Calgary, 2004–10. Held several portfolios in Stephen Harper's government. Progressive Conservative premier of Alberta, 2014–15.

Rae, Bob (1948–): NDP premier of Ontario, 1990–95. Later became a Liberal and ran for the leadership of the party but was defeated by Michael Ignatieff. Canada's ambassador to the United Nations since 2020.

Rock, Allan (1947–): Liberal MP for Etobicoke Centre, ON, 1993–2004. Served as minister of justice and minister of health under Jean Chrétien. Prominent lawyer.

Scheer, Andrew (1979–): Leader of the Conservative Party, 2017–20. Before becoming leader, was a Conservative MP and then speaker of the House of Commons. Forced out as leader in 2020 after the Conservatives under his leadership won more votes but fewer seats than the Liberals.

Singh, Jagmeet (1979–): Leader of the NDP, 2017–. Previously sat in the Ontario Provincial Parliament.

Solberg, Monte (1958–): Reform/Canadian Alliance/Conservative MP from Medicine Hat, AB, 1993–2008. Served briefly in Stephen Harper's cabinet before retiring to become a political consultant.

St. Laurent, Louis (1882–1973): Liberal prime minister of Canada, 1948–1957. Had been a lawyer in Quebec until he was elected as a Liberal MP in a 1942 by-election. Served as minister of justice and secretary of state for external affairs in Mackenzie King's cabinet.

Stanfield, Robert (1914–2003): Progressive Conservative premier of Nova Scotia, 1956–67, and leader of the federal Progressive Conservative Party, 1967–76. Led three unsuccessful campaigns against Pierre Trudeau, although he came very close to winning in 1972.

Strahl, Chuck (1957–): Reform/Canadian Alliance/Conservative MP from British Columbia, 1993–2011. Held several positions in Stephen Harper's government.

Stronach, Belinda (1966–): Daughter of auto-parts magnate Frank Stronach. Opposed Stephen Harper for the leadership of the Conservative Party of Canada in 2004. Elected to Parliament as a Conservative in 2004; defected to the Liberals in 2005 and briefly served as a cabinet minister. Retained her Commons seat as a Liberal in 2006 but did not run again in 2008.

Stronach, Frank (1932–): Immigrant from Austria, billionaire founder of Magna International auto-parts company.

Tory, John (1954–): Manager of the PC war room in the 1993 election campaign. Formerly a prominent Toronto businessman and Progressive Conservative worker. Later became leader of the Ontario Progressive Conservative Party, 2004–09, and mayor of Toronto, 2014–.

Trudeau, Justin (1971–): Son of former prime minister Pierre Trudeau and himself Liberal prime minister of Canada, 2015–. Educated at McGill University and the University of British Columbia. Worked as a secondary school teacher and motivational speaker until he entered politics in 2008, winning the seat of Papineau, Quebec, for the Liberals. Re-elected in 2011 and then became Liberal leader in 2013. Led the Liberals to a majority government in 2015, and his government was returned to power in the elections of 2019 and 2021 with a minority of seats.

Trudeau, Pierre Elliott (1919–2000): Liberal prime minister of Canada, 1968–79 and 1980–84. Former journalist and law professor. Was recruited to run for the Liberals in 1965. Became party leader in 1968 and proceeded to win four elections, losing narrowly in 1979 to the Progressive Conservatives led by Joe Clark. His government was responsible for important policy innovations such as official bilingualism and the Canadian Charter of Rights and Freedoms. Opposed the Meech Lake and

Charlottetown Accords, even though he was retired, because he thought they would weaken the federal government and encourage Quebec nationalism.

Turner, John (1929–2020): Liberal prime minister of Canada, 1984. First elected as a Liberal MP in 1968. Served as minister of justice and minister of finance, then left politics in 1975. Returned to win the Liberal leadership in 1984, which briefly made him prime minister. Led the Liberals to defeat in 1984 and again in 1988, though they won more seats in the latter year. Retired as leader in 1990 and did not seek re-election in 1993.

Wells, Clyde (1937–): Liberal Premier of Newfoundland, 1989–96. Scuttled the Meech Lake Accord by refusing to hold a ratification vote in the legislature. After retiring from politics, was appointed a justice of the Court of Appeal for Newfound and Labrador and later chief justice.

White, Bob (1935–2017): President of the Canadian Labour Congress at the time of the 1993 election. Previously president of the Canadian Auto Workers. Known as an opponent of free trade with the United States.

Wilson, Michael (1937–2019): Progressive Conservative MP from Ontario, 1979–93. Minister of finance under Brian Mulroney, 1984–91. Later served as minister of international trade and minister of industry, science, and technology, 1991–93, helping to negotiate the North American Free Trade Agreement. Investment executive in Toronto.

Appendix 2
Timeline of Events

1980

February 18   The Liberals, led by Pierre Trudeau, are elected to a majority government. The Progressive Conservatives are reduced to one seat in Quebec.

1981

November 4   The federal government and nine provinces approve constitutional amendments, including the Charter of Rights and Freedoms, without Quebec's agreement, laying the groundwork for future disputes.

1982

April 17   Queen Elizabeth II signs the Constitution Act, 1982, which includes the Charter of Rights and Freedoms. The Canadian constitution is now "patriated," still without the support of Quebec.

1983

June 11   Brian Mulroney is chosen leader of the Progressive Conservative Party of Canada, defeating previous leader Joe Clark. Mulroney has promised to greatly increase the Conservative vote in Quebec.

1984

June 16   John Turner defeats Jean Chrétien to become leader of the Liberal Party, replacing Pierre Trudeau, who has announced his retirement. Turner serves as prime minister until the Liberals are defeated three months later in the 1984 election.

September 11   Progressive Conservatives led by Brian Mulroney win a landslide victory in the national election and proceed to form a majority government.

1987

April 30   Prime Minister Mulroney and ten provincial premiers agree up the Meech Lake Accord.

May 29–31   The Western Assembly on Canada's Economic and Political Future is held in Vancouver. It leads to the formation of the Reform Party of Canada.

November 1   Preston Manning is acclaimed as leader of the Reform Party of Canada at its founding convention in Winnipeg.

1988

November 21   The Progressive Conservatives are returned to office with a reduced but still strong majority.

1989

December 2   Audrey McLaughlin wins the leadership of the New Democratic Party.

1990

June 23   The Meech Lake Accord dies because of the failure of ratification by the legislative assemblies of Manitoba and Newfoundland.

June 23   Jean Chrétien defeats Paul Martin and Sheila Copps at a Liberal leadership convention, thereby becoming leader of the opposition in the House of Commons.

1992

August 28   The text of the Charlottetown Accord is approved by the prime minister and the premiers of nine provinces, but the premier of Quebec is neutral.

October 26   The Charlottetown Accord is defeated in a national referendum.

1993

February 24   Brian Mulroney announces that he will retire as prime minister and will not seek re-election to Parliament.

June 25   Kim Campbell becomes prime minister of Canada after defeating Jean Charest in the Progressive Conservative leadership race.

September 8   Prime Minister Kim Campbell requests a dissolution of Parliament, and a national election campaign begins. Campbell makes her first big gaffe, saying unemployment may remain high till the turn of the century.

September 12   The Liberals release their campaign platform known as the Red Book.

September 20   Preston Manning re-releases Reform's Zero-in-Three plan for balancing the federal budget.

September 23   Campbell says issues are too complex to discuss during a campaign. Afterwards, Conservative support starts to slide while support for the Liberals, Reform, and BQ goes up.

October 3–4   Leaders' debates are held, first in French, then in English. Campbell fails to turn things around, appears not to know the size of the federal budget deficit.

October 15   Conservative campaign releases anti-Chrétien attack ads, which backfire badly. Conservative support falls even further.

October 25   The Liberals led by Jean Chrétien win a majority
                  government. The Bloc Québécois and the Reform
                  Party each win over fifty seats, with the Bloc form-
                  ing the official opposition. The Progressive Con-
                  servatives are reduced to two seats, and the NDP
                  to nine.

1997

June 2   The Liberals, led by Jean Chrétien, win another
                  majority in the national election. The Reform Party
                  becomes the official opposition.

2000

March 27   The Reform Party transforms itself into the Can-
                  adian Alliance, absorbing some provincial Conserv-
                  atives, but the federal Progressive Conservative
                  Party stays aloof.

June 24   Stockwell Day defeats Preston Manning to become
                  leader of the Canadian Alliance.

November 27   The Liberals, led by Jean Chrétien, win another ma-
                  jority government. The Canadian Alliance makes
                  only small gains over what Reform had achieved.

2002

March 20   Stephen Harper defeats Stockwell Day to become
                  leader of the Canadian Alliance.

November 14   Paul Martin defeats Sheila Copps to become leader
                  of the Liberal Party of Canada.

2003

December 7   Conservative Party of Canada is founded as a
                  merger of the Canadian Alliance and the Progressive
                  Conservative Party of Canada.

December 12   Paul Martin becomes prime minister of Canada.

2004

March 20   Stephen Harper wins leadership of the new Con-
                  servative Party of Canada.

June 28	The Liberals, led by Paul Martin, are reduced to a minority government.

2005

November 28	Paul Martin's Liberal government is defeated on a vote of non-confidence; national election ensues.

2006

January 23	The Conservative Party of Canada wins more seats than the Liberals in a national election. Paul Martin resigns and Stephen Harper becomes prime minister.

2008

October 14	The Conservatives, led by Stephen Harper, win another minority government against the Liberals, led by Stéphane Dion.

2011

May 2	The Conservatives, led by Stephen Harper, win a majority government. The NDP, led by Jack Layton, wins 103 seats and becomes official opposition. The Bloc Québécois is reduced to 4 seats.
August 22	NDP leader Jack Layton dies of cancer.

2013

April 14	Justin Trudeau wins the Liberal leadership race.

2015

October 19	The Liberals, led by Justin Trudeau, win majority of seats. Conservative leader Stephen Harper resigns.

2019

October 21	The Liberals, led by Justin Trudeau, are returned to power but with a minority government. The Conservatives, led by Andrew Scheer, win more votes than the Liberals but fewer seats. The Bloc Québécois recovers to win thirty-two seats while the NDP falls to twenty-four.

2021

September 20 The Liberals, led by Justin Trudeau, win another minority government. Vote shares and number of seats for all major parties remain similar to the results of the 2019 election.

2022

March 21 The Liberals and NDP announce confidence-and-supply agreement, creating a two-party working majority in the House of Commons.

Notes

Preface

1 Tom Flanagan, *Waiting for the Wave: The Reform Party and the Conservative Movement* (Montreal and Kingston: McGill-Queen's University Press, 2009).

2 Tom Flanagan, *Harper's Team: Behind the Scenes in the Conservative Rise to Power* (Montreal and Kingston: McGill-Queen's University Press, 2007). Harper disapproved of my writing the book and sent me into political exile, at least as far as the Conservative Party was concerned. I had a talent for falling out with the leaders I worked for.

3 T.S. Eliot, *The Complete Poems and Plays, 1909–1950* (New York: Harcourt, Brace, and World, 1952), 128.

4 Tom Flanagan, "The Concept of Fortuna in Machiavelli," in *The Political Calculus,* edited by A. Parel, 127–56 (Toronto: University of Toronto Press, 1972).

5 Eliot, *Complete Poems and Plays,* 129.

Introduction

1 John C. Courtney, *Revival and Change: The 1957 and 1958 Diefenbaker Elections* (Vancouver: UBC Press, 2022).

2 Canada, House of Commons, *Members By-Law*, March 25, 2021, section 1(1), https://www.ourcommons.ca/DocumentViewer/en/boie/by-law/10000.

3 Alan C. Cairns, "The Electoral System and the Party System in Canada, 1921–1965," *Canadian Journal of Political Science* 1, 1 (1968): 55–80.

4 Wikipedia, s.v. "List of Canadian Federal General Elections," February 28, 2022, https://en.wikipedia.org/wiki/List_of_Canadian_federal_general_elections.

5 R. Kenneth Carty and William Cross, "Political Parties and the Practice of Brokerage Politics," in *The Oxford Handbook of Canadian Politics*, edited by John C. Courtney and David Smith (Toronto: Oxford University Press, 2010).

6 R. Kenneth Carty, William Cross, and Lisa Young, *Rebuilding Canadian Party Politics* (Vancouver: UBC Press, 2000).

Chapter 1: Grand Coalition

1 This introductory section is based on Tom Flanagan, *Winning Power: Canadian Campaigning in the Twenty-First Century* (Montreal and Kingston: McGill-Queen's University Press, 2014), 11–15.

2 Frans de Waal, *Chimpanzee Politics: Power and Sex among Apes* (Baltimore: Johns Hopkins University Press, 1982).

3 Frans de Waal, *Bonobo: The Forgotten Ape* (Berkeley: University of California Press, 1997).

4 Mark O. Dickerson, Thomas Flanagan, and Brenda O'Neill, *An Introduction to Government and Politics: A Conceptual Approach*, 8th ed. (Toronto: Nelson, 2010), 9–10.

5 Claude Bélanger, "Quebec and Federal Elections, 1867–2006," Quebec History, Marianopolis College, Montreal, August 2008, http://faculty.marianopolis.edu/c.belanger/QuebecHistory/readings/fedelect.htm.

6 R. Kenneth Carty, *Big Tent Politics: The Liberal Party's Long Mastery of Canada's Public Life* (Vancouver: UBC Press, 2015), 17.

7 Conrad Black, *Duplessis* (Toronto: McClelland and Stewart, 1977), 404–9.

8 Carty, *Big Tent Politics*, 23.

9 Quoted in L. Ian MacDonald, *The Making of the Prime Minister* (Toronto: McClelland and Stewart, 1984), 201.

10 *Re: Objection by Quebec to a Resolution to amend the Constitution*, [1982] 2 SCR 793.

11 Quoted in MacDonald, *The Making of the Prime Minister*, 289.

12 André Bernard, "The Bloc Québécois," in *The Canadian General Election of 1993*, edited by Alan Frizzell, Jon H. Pammett, and Anthony Westell (Ottawa: Carleton University Press, 1994), 80.

13 Carty, *Big Tent Politics*, 45.

14 Thomas Flanagan, *Game Theory and Canadian Politics* (Toronto: University of Toronto Press, 1998), 76–92.

15 James Rose, "Remember When? Alberta's Economy under Trudeau (Sr.)," *BOE Report*, October 6, 2015, https://boereport.com/2015/10/06/remember-when-albertas-economy-and-trudeau-the-elder/.

16 Robert Axelrod, *Conflict of Interest: A Theory of Divergent Goals with Application to Politics* (Chicago: Markham, 1970), 167–83.

17 David J. Bercuson, J.L. Granatstein, and W.R. Young, *Sacred Trust: Brian Mulroney and the Conservative Party in Power* (Toronto: Doubleday, 1987).

18 Charlie Mayer, "Liberals Should Take a Cue from Mulroney, Not Chrétien," *National Post*, May 20, 2020, https://nationalpost.com/opinion/charlie-mayer-liberals-should-take-a-cue-from-mulroney-not-chretien.

19 "Inflation Canada 1980," Worldwide Inflation Data, https://www.inflation.eu/inflation-rates/canada/historic-inflation/cpi-inflation-canada-1980.aspx.

20 Quoted in Preston Manning, *The New Canada* (Toronto: Macmillan Canada, 1992), 127.

21 Brian Mulroney, *Memoirs: 1939–1993* (Toronto: McClelland and Stewart, 2007), 481–82.

22 David R. Elliot and Iris Miller, *Bible Bill: A Biography of William Aberhart* (Edmonton: Reidmore Books, 1987).

23 *The Constitution Act, 1867*, 30 & 31 Vict, c 3, s 91 (14–21), CanLII, https://canlii.ca/t/ldsw.

24 Tom Flanagan and Martha Lee, "From Social Credit to Social Conservatism: The Evolution of an Ideology," *Prairie Forum* 16 (1991): 205–23.

25 E.C. Manning, *Political Realignment: A Challenge to Thoughtful Canadians* (Toronto: McClelland and Stewart, 1967).

26 Ted Byfield, ed., *Act of Faith* (Vancouver: British Columbia Report Books, 1991).

27 For details, see William Johnson, *Stephen Harper and the Future of Canada* (Toronto: Random House, 2005); and John Ibbitson, *Stephen Harper* (Toronto: McClelland and Stewart, 2016).

28 Michael Rose, "What Bourassa Won," *Maclean's*, May 11, 1987, https://archive.macleans.ca/article/1987/5/11/what-bourassa-won.

29 "Pierre Trudeau Calls Mulroney a 'Weakling' over Meech Lake," *CBC Radio*, May 31, 1987, https://www.cbc.ca/archives/entry/meech-lake-is-mulroney-a-weakling.

30 Brian Mulroney, *Where I Stand* (Toronto: McClelland and Stewart, 1983).

31 Richard Johnston, André Blais, Henry Brady, and Jean Crête, *Letting the People Decide: The Dynamics of Canadian Elections* (Montreal and Kingston: McGill-Queen's University Press, 1992).

32 Quoted in Tom Flanagan, *Waiting for the Wave: The Reform Party and Preston Manning* (Toronto: Stoddart, 1995), 59.

Chapter 2: Collapse of the Coalition

1 Ted Byfield, ed., *Act of Faith* (Vancouver: British Columbia Report Books, 1991), 65–69.

2 Byfield, *Act of Faith*, 72–75.

3 Astrid Lange, "History of the GST," *Toronto Star,* January 1, 2008.

4 *Ford v Quebec (Attorney General),* [1988] 2 SCR 712, https://scc-csc.lexum.com/scc-csc/scc-csc/en/item/384/index.do.

5 "Jean Charest," McCarthy Tétrault, https://www.mccarthy.ca/en/people/jean-charest.

6 L. Ian MacDonald, *From Bourassa to Bourassa: Wilderness to Restoration,* 2nd ed. (Montreal and Kingston: McGill-Queen's University Press, 2002), 302–3.

7 Lawrence Martin, *The Antagonist: Lucien Bouchard and the Politics of Delusion* (Toronto: Viking, 1997).

8 Peter C. Newman, *The Secret Mulroney Tapes: Unguarded Confessions of a Prime Minister* (Toronto: Random House Canada, 2005), 172.

9 Lucien Bouchard, *On the Record,* translated by Dominique Clift (Toronto: Stoddart, 1994), 256.

10 Pierre Trudeau, Speech at the Paul Sauvé Arena, Montreal, May 14, 1980 (translation), https://canadahistory.ca/sections/documents/leaders/Trudeau/Speech%20at%20Paul%20Sauve%20Arena%20May%2014%201980.htm.

11 Tom Flanagan, *Waiting for the Wave: The Reform Party and Preston Manning* (Toronto: Stoddart, 1995), 105–6.

12 David B. Magleby, "Opinion Formation and Opinion Change in Ballot Proposition Campaigns," in *Manipulating Public Opinion: Essays on Public Opinion as Dependent Variable,* edited by Michael Margolis and Gary A. Mauser (Pacific Grove, CA: Brooks/Cole, 1989), 112.

13 Joe Clark, *A Nation Too Good to Lose: Renewing the Purpose of Canada* (Toronto: Key Porter, 1994), 123.

14 Richard Johnston, "The Inverted Logroll: The Charlottetown Accord and the Referendum," *PS: Political Science and Politics* 26 (March 1993): 43–48.

15 *Referendum Act,* SC 1992, c 30, https://laws-lois.justice.gc.ca/eng/acts/R-4.7/page-1.html.

16 Richard Johnston, André Blais, Elisabeth Gidengil, and Neil Nevitte, *The Challenge of Direct Democracy: The 1992 Canadian Referendum* (Montreal and Kingston: McGill-Queen's University Press, 1996), 148–49.

17 Pierre Elliott Trudeau, *Trudeau: "A Mess That Deserves a Big NO"* (Toronto: Robert Davies Publishing, 1992).

18 Tom Flanagan, "The Staying Power of the Legislative Status Quo: Collective Choice in Canada's Parliament after Morgentaler," *Canadian Journal of Political Science* 30 (1997): 31–53.

19 David McLaughlin, *Poisoned Chalice: The Last Campaign of the Progressive Conservative Party?* (Toronto: Dundurn, 1994), 29.

20 Martin, *The Antagonist,* 240.

21 Flanagan, *Waiting for the Wave,* 124.

22 Kim Campbell, *Time and Chance: The Political Memoirs of Canada's First Woman Prime Minister* (Toronto: Doubleday Canada, 1996), 256.

23 Barbara Woodley (photographer), "The Honourable Kim Campbell, Minister of Justice and Attorney General of Canada," July 30, 1990, Library and Archives Canada, Photographs/Portraits, box SC 0575, item 3518825, https://central.bac-lac.gc.ca/.redirect?app=fonandcol&id=3518825&lang=eng.

24 Peter C. Newman, *The Secret Mulroney Tapes* (Toronto: Random House Canada, 2005), 429.

25 Campbell, *Time and Chance,* 290.

26 Linda Trimble, *Ms. Prime Minister: Gender, Media, and Leadership* (Toronto: University of Toronto Press, 2017), 40–41.

27 Ecclesiastes 9:11 KJV. Bible Gateway, https://www.biblegateway.com/passage/?search=Ecclesiastes%209:11&version=KJV.

28 Brian Mulroney, *Memoirs: 1939–1993* (Toronto: McClelland and Stewart, 2007), 108–10.

29 McLaughlin, *Poisoned Chalice,* 141–42.

30 Trimble, *Ms. Prime Minister,* 158.

Chapter 3: The Contestants

1 Aristotle, *Rhetoric,* 1356a, cited in Richard McKeon, ed., *The Basic Works of Aristotle* (New York: Random House, 1941), 1329; Tom Flanagan,

Winning Power: Canadian Campaigning in the 21st Century (Montreal and Kingston: McGill-Queen's University Press, 2014), 20.

2 Flanagan, *Winning Power,* 118.

3 Clare Buckley, *Moving Pieces: A Comparison of Canadian Provincial Party Platforms* (MA thesis, University of Alberta, 2020), 4–6, https://era.library.ualberta.ca/items/63e563d3-930e-4c5d-93f2-ca8d1e689238.

4 Joan Bryden, "Trudeau Pledges to End First-Past-the-Post Electoral System if Elected," *CTV News,* June 16, 2015, https://winnipeg.ctvnews.ca/trudeau-pledges-to-end-first-past-the-post-electoral-system-if-elected-1.2424905.

5 Mel Hurtig, *The Betrayal of Canada* (Toronto: Stoddart, 1991).

6 "History," The Council of Canadians, https://canadians.org/history.

7 "Follow the Money – Highlights," *National Post,* December 15, 2020, https://nationalpost.com/news/politics/follow-the-money-highlights.

8 Tom Flanagan, *Waiting for the Wave: The Reform Party and Preston Manning* (Toronto: Stoddart, 1995), 124.

9 The 1993 *Blue Book* can be found in some libraries but is not available online. Its contents are summarized in Dick Field, "A Look Back at the Reform Party Blue Book," *Canada Free Press,* April 1, 2012, https://canadafreepress.com/article/a-look-back-at-the-reform-party-blue-book.

10 Stephen Harper, Speech in the House of Commons, February 19, 2003, Open Parliament, https://openparliament.ca/debates/2003/2/19/stephen-harper-4/only/#:~:text=Preston%20Manning%20used%20to%20say%20that%20the%20best,on%20a%20plan%20that%20went%20over%20three%20years.

11 "The Only Deficit Plan We've Seen," *Globe and Mail,* September 23, 1993, quoted in Flanagan, *Waiting for the Wave,* 146.

12 Quoted in Ian McLeod, *Under Siege: The Federal NDP in the Nineties* (Toronto: James Lorimer, 1994), 25.

13 Quoted in McLeod, *Under Siege,* 34.

14 Alan Whitehorn, "The NDP's Quest for Survival," in *The Canadian General Election of 1993,* edited by Alan Frizzell, Jon H. Pammett, and Anthony Westell (Ottawa: Carleton University Press, 1994), 43–50.

15 Audrey McLaughlin, *A Woman's Place: My Life and Politics* (Toronto: McFarlane, Walter, and Ross, 1992).

16 McLeod, *Under Siege,* 106.

17 McLeod, *Under Siege,* 100.

18 McLeod, *Under Siege,* 107.

19 Lawrence Martin, *The Antagonist: Lucien Bouchard and the Politics of Delusion* (Toronto: Viking, 1997), 245.

20 Martin, *The Antagonist.*

21 Greg Weston, *Reign of Error: The Inside Story of John Turner's Troubled Leadership* (Toronto: McGraw-Hill Ryerson, 1988).

22 Brooke Jeffrey, *Divided Loyalties: The Liberal Party of Canada, 1984–2008* (Toronto: University of Toronto Press, 2010).

23 "A Very Bitter Defeat for Paul Martin," *CBC Archives,* June 23, 1990, https://www.cbc.ca/archives/entry/a-very-bitter-defeat-for-paul-martin.

24 Sheila Copps, *Worth Fighting For* (Toronto: McClelland and Stewart, 2004), 172.

25 Susan Delacourt, *Juggernaut: Paul Martin's Campaign for Chrétien's Crown* (Toronto: McClelland and Stewart, 2003).

26 Copps, *Worth Fighting For,* 198–208.

27 Jeffrey, *Divided Loyalties,* 225–27.

28 Lawrence Martin, *Iron Man: The Defiant Reign of Jean Chrétien,* vol. 2 (Toronto: Viking Canada, 2003), 60.

29 Stephen Clarkson, "Yesterday's Man and His Blue Grits: Backward into the Future," in *The Canadian General Election of 1993,* edited by Alan Frizzell, Jon H. Pammett, and Anthony Westell (Ottawa: Carleton University Press, 1994), 33–34.

30 Clarkson, "Yesterday's Man," 32.

31 David McLaughlin, *Poisoned Chalice: The Last Campaign of the Progressive Conservative Party?* (Toronto: Dundurn, 1994), 142.

32 Kim Campbell, *Time and Chance: The Political Memoirs of Canada's First Woman Prime Minister* (Toronto: Doubleday Canada, 1996), 258.

33 McLaughlin, *Poisoned Chalice,* 131.

34 Campbell, *Time and Chance,* 284.

35 Campbell, *Time and Chance,* 286.

36 Details in Tom Flanagan, *Harper's Team: Behind the Scenes in the Conservative Rise to Power* (Montreal and Kingston: McGill-Queen's University Press, 2007), 163–227.

37 Richard Johnston, André Blais, Henry Brady, and Jean Crête, *Letting the People Decide: The Dynamics of Canadian Elections* (Montreal and Kingston: McGill-Queen's University Press, 1992), 132.

38 Elections Canada, *Thirty-Fifth General Election, 1993: Contributions and Expenses of Registered Political Parties and Candidates* (Ottawa: Chief Electoral Officer of Canada, 1993), 3, Table 12.

39 John Laschinger, *Campaign Confessions* (Toronto: Dundurn, 2016).
40 Stephen Brooks, *Canadian Democracy,* 2nd ed. (Toronto: Oxford University Press, 1996), 208.

Chapter 4: The Contest

1 Lawrence LeDuc and Jon H. Pammett, *Dynasties and Interludes: Past and Present in Canadian Electoral Politics,* 2nd ed. (Toronto: Dundurn, 2016), Table 11.3.
2 David McLaughlin, *Poisoned Chalice: The Last Campaign of the Progressive Conservative Party?* (Toronto: Dundurn, 1994), 179.
3 Conquest Research, September 14, 1993, cited in Anthony Wilson-Smith, "A Struggle to Survive," *Maclean's,* October 18, 1993, https://archive.macleans.ca/issue/19931018#!&pid=14.
4 Clare Buckley, *Moving Pieces: A Comparison of Canadian Provincial Party Platforms* (MA thesis, University of Alberta, 2020), 6, https://era.library.ualberta.ca/items/63e563d3-930e-4c5d-93f2-ca8d1e689238.
5 Tom Flanagan, *Winning Power: Canadian Campaigning in the Twenty-First Century* (Montreal and Kingston: McGill-Queen's University Press, 2014), 80–88.
6 Kim Campbell, *Time and Chance: The Political Memoirs of Canada's First Woman Prime Minister* (Toronto: Doubleday Canada, 1996), 366.
7 Campbell, *Time and Chance,* 367–68.
8 McLaughlin, *Poisoned Chalice,* 210.
9 Tom Flanagan, *Waiting for the Wave: The Reform Party and Preston Manning* (Toronto: Stoddart, 1995), 144; McLaughlin, *Poisoned Chalice,* 213.
10 McLaughlin, *Poisoned Chalice,* 217.
11 Quoted in Flanagan, *Waiting for the Wave,* 145.
12 Quoted in Flanagan, *Waiting for the Wave,* 146.
13 McLaughlin, *Poisoned Chalice,* 229.
14 Lawrence LeDuc, "The Leaders' Debates," in *The Canadian General Election of 1993,* edited by Alan Frizzell, Jon H. Pammett, and Anthony Westell (Ottawa: Carleton University Press, 1994), 135.
15 LeDuc, "The Leaders' Debates," 129.
16 Campbell, *Time and Chance,* 380.
17 McLaughlin, *Poisoned Chalice,* 233.
18 The ad can be seen at https://www.youtube.com/watch?v=D000Amn9CIA.

19 Walter I. Romanow, Michel de Repentigny, Stanley B. Cunningham, Walter C. Soderlund, and Kai Hildebrandt, *Television Advertising in Canadian Elections: The Attack Mode, 1993* (Waterloo, ON: Wilfrid Laurier University Press, 1999), 33.

20 Stephen Clarkson, "Yesterday's Man and His Blue Grits: Backward into the Future," in *The Canadian General Election of 1993*, edited by Alan Frizzell, Jon H. Pammett, and Anthony Westell (Ottawa: Carleton University Press, 1994), 37.

21 McLaughlin, *Poisoned Chalice*, 258.

22 McLaughlin, *Poisoned Chalice*, 259.

23 Romanow et al., *Television Advertising*, 43.

24 "An Unforgettable Fumble for Robert Stanfield," *CBC Archives*, June 2, 2004, https://www.cbc.ca/archives/entry/an-unforgettable-fumble -for-robert-stanfield; Haroon Siddiqui, "Mitt Romney's Joe Clark Moment of Failed Gravitas," *Toronto Star*, August 1, 2012, https://www.thestar.com/ opinion/editorialopinion/2012/08/01/mitt_romneys_joe_clark_ moment_of_failed_gravitas.html; Flanagan, *Waiting for the Wave*, 149–52.

25 Flanagan, *Waiting for the Wave*, 152.

26 Cited in Flanagan, *Waiting for the Wave*, 152.

27 Preston Manning, *Think Big: My Life in Politics* (Toronto: McClelland and Stewart, 2003), 86.

28 André Bernard, "The Bloc Québécois," in *The Canadian General Election of 1993*, edited by Alan Frizzell, Jon H. Pammett, and Anthony Westell (Ottawa: Carleton University Press, 1994), 85.

29 The term "bozo eruption" is appropriately descriptive but a bit anachronistic here. The earlier term "bimbo eruption" goes back to Bill Clinton's 1992 US presidential campaign. "Bozo eruption" came into currency in Canada with 2004 Conservative campaign. Stuart Thomson, "Violent Ejections of Idiocy: A People's History of 'Bozo Eruptions' in Canada," *National Post*, January 2, 2019, https://nationalpost.com/news/politics/ violent-ejections-of-idiocy-a-peoples-history-of-bozo-eruptions-in -canada.

30 Thomson, "Violent Ejections of Idiocy."

31 Lawrence Martin, *The Antagonist: Lucien Bouchard and the Politics of Delusion* (Toronto: Viking, 1997), 245.

32 Martin, *The Antagonist*, 246.

33 Ian McLeod, *Under Siege: The Federal NDP in the Nineties* (Toronto: James Lorimer, 1994), 100–4.

34 Romanow et al., *Television Advertising,* 40.

35 Alan Whitehorn, "The NDP's Quest for Survival," in *The Canadian General Election of 1993,* edited by Alan Frizzell, Jon H. Pammett, and Anthony Westell (Ottawa: Carleton University Press, 1994), 49.

36 McLeod, *Under Siege,* 109.

37 Lawrence Martin, *Iron Man: The Defiant Reign of Jean Chrétien,* vol. 2 (Toronto: Viking Canada, 2003), 63.

38 Martin, *Iron Man,* 65; Warren Kinsella, *Kicking Ass in Canadian Politics* (Toronto: Random House, 2001).

39 Stephen Clarkson, *The Big Red Machine: How the Liberal Party Dominates Canadian Politics* (Vancouver: UBC Press, 2005), 169.

40 Romanow et al., *Television Advertising,* 36.

41 Brook Jeffrey, *Divided Loyalties: The Liberal Party of Canada, 1984–2008* (Toronto: University of Toronto Press, 2010), 230.

42 *Creating Opportunity: The Liberal Plan for Canada* (1993), https://web.archive.org/web/19961109135723/http://www.liberal.ca/english/policy/red_book/chapter1.html.

43 Sheila Copps, *Worth Fighting For* (Toronto: McClelland and Stewart, 2004), 112.

44 McLaughlin, *Poisoned Chalice,* 241–42.

45 Alan Frizzell and Anthony Westell, "The Press and the Prime Minister," in *The Canadian General Election of 1993,* edited by Alan Frizzell, Jon H. Pammett, and Anthony Westell (Ottawa: Carleton University Press, 1994), 96.

46 Linda Trimble, *Ms. Prime Minister: Gender, Media, and Leadership* (Toronto: University of Toronto Press, 2017), 189.

47 "Voter Turnout at Federal Elections and Referendums," Elections Canada, https://www.elections.ca/content.aspx?section=ele&dir=turn&document=index&lang=e. The figure of 70.9 percent is adjusted from the raw figure of 69.6 percent because in all provinces except Quebec a year-old voters' list from the 1992 referendum was employed.

48 "Voter Turnout at Federal Elections," Elections Canada.

49 LeDuc and Pammett, *Dynasties and Interludes,* ch. 1.

50 V.O. Key, "A Theory of Critical Elections," *Journal of Politics* 17 (1955): 3–18.

51 LeDuc and Pammett, *Dynasties and Interludes,* ch. 1.

52 *Free Dictionary,* s.v., "Close enough for government work," https://idioms. thefreedictionary.com/close+enough+for+government+work.

53 Maurice Duverger, *Political Parties: Their Organization and Activity in the Modern State,* translated by Barbara and Robert North (New York: John Wiley and Sons, 1954).

54 Jon H. Pammett, "Tracking the Votes," in *The Canadian General Election of 1993,* edited by Alan Frizzell, Jon H. Pammett, and Anthony Westell (Ottawa: Carleton University Press, 1994), 146.

55 "[New Jersey is like] a beer barrel, tapped at both ends, with all the live beer running into Philadelphia and New York," LibQuotes, https:// libquotes.com/benjamin-franklin/quote/lbw1o4v.

56 John Spacey, "What Is Abductive Reasoning?" Simplicable, July 14, 2017, https://simplicable.com/new/abductive-reasoning#:~:text=Abductive% 20reasoning,%20or%20abduction,%20is%20a%20form%20of,doesn't%20 guarantee%20that%20a%20theory%20is%20logically%20correct.

Chapter 5: Aftermath

1 Lawrence Martin, *The Antagonist: Lucien Bouchard and the Politics of Delusion* (Toronto: Viking, 1997), 257.

2 Tom Flanagan, *Waiting for the Wave: The Reform Party and Preston Manning* (Toronto: Stoddart, 1995), 31–32.

3 Colin Craig, "Taxpayers Federation Honours Preston Manning, Werner Schmidt and Lee Morrison with TaxFighter Award," Canadian Taxpayers Federation news release, June 20, 2013, https://www.taxpayer.com/news -room-archive/Taxpayers%20Federation%20Honours%20Preston %20Manning,%20Werner%20Schmidt%20and%20Lee%20Morrison% 20with%20TaxFighter%20Award.

4 Department of Finance Canada, *Fiscal Reference Tables, 1999,* https://www. canada.ca/content/dam/fin/migration/afr-rfa/1999/frt99e.pdf.

5 Jean Chrétien, *My Years as Prime Minister* (Toronto: Alfred A. Knopf Canada, 2007), 50.

6 Paul Martin, *The Budget in Brief* (Ottawa: Department of Finance Canada,1994), https://www.budget.gc.ca/pdfarch/1994-brf-eng.pdf.

7 "Value of 1993 Canadian Dollar Today," InflationTool, https://www. inflationtool.com/canadian-dollar/1993-to-present-value.

8   Lawrence Martin, *Iron Man: The Defiant Reign of Jean Chrétien,* vol. 2 (Toronto: Viking Canada, 2003), 98.

9   Niels Veldhuis, "Message from the Institute's President," *The Quarterly* (Fraser Institute), April 2020, back of front cover.

10 Details in Eddie Goldenberg, *The Way It Works: Inside Ottawa* (Toronto: McClelland and Stewart, 2007), chs. 7–8; Donald Savoie, *Governing from the Centre: The Concentration of Power in Canadian Politics* (Toronto: University of Toronto Press, 1999).

11 Herb Grubel, *A Professor in Parliament: Experiencing a Turbulent Parliament and Reform Party Caucus, 1993–97* (West Vancouver: Gordon Soules, 2000), 255.

12 "Election Expenses and Reimbursements, by Registered Political Party – 1997 General Election," Elections Canada, https://elections.ca/content. aspx?section=fin&document=exp_reim_1997&dir=oth/pol/remb &lang=e.

13 Wikipedia, s.v., "Stephen Harper," last modified June 17, 2022, https:// en.wikipedia.org/wiki/Stephen_Harper.

14 Rick Salutin, "The New Sherriff's First Week in Town," *Globe and Mail,* September 22, 2000, https://www.theglobeandmail.com/news/national/ the-new-sheriffs-first-week-in-town/article769978/.

15 "Election Expenses and Reimbursements, by Registered Political Party – 2000 General Election," Elections Canada, https://elections.ca/content. aspx?section=fin&dir=oth/pol/remb&document=table1&lang=e.

16 Tom Flanagan, *Harper's Team: Behind the Scenes in the Conservative Rise to Power* (Montreal and Kingston: McGill-Queen's University Press, 2007), 28–65.

17 Flanagan, *Harper's Team,* 97–136.

18 "Paris vaut bien une messe," Linternaute.com, http://www.linternaute. fr/expression/langue-francaise/6723/paris-vaut-bien-une-messe/.

19 Tom Flanagan, "Stephen Harper and the N-Word," *Maclean's,* December 11, 2006. https://archive.macleans.ca/article/2006/12/11/harper-and -the-n-word.

20 Mario Cardinal, *Breaking Point, Quebec–Canada: The 1995 Referendum* (Montreal: Bayard Canada Books, 2005).

21 David McGrane, *The New NDP: Moderation, Modernization, and Political Marketing* (Vancouver: UBC Press, 2019).

22 McGrane, *New NDP,* 217.

23 McGrane, *New NDP,* 241–45.

24 McGrane, *New NDP,* 260.

25 Bill 21, *An Act respecting the laicity of the state,* 1st Sess, 42nd Leg, Quebec, 2019 (assented to June 16, 2019), SQ 2019, c 12, http://www2.publications duquebec.gouv.qc.ca/dynamicSearch/telecharge.php?type=5&file= 2019C12A.PDF.

26 Teddy Elliott, "Jagmeet Singh Appears without a Turban & Discusses Identity in New French Campaign Video," *Mtl Blog,* September 4, 2019, https://www.mtlblog.com/news/canada/qc/montreal/jagmeet -singh-appears-without-a-turban-and-discusses-identity-in-new-french -campaign-video.

Chapter 6: The Punctuated Equilibrium of Canadian Politics

1 *Biology Dictionary,* s.v. "Punctuated Equilibrium," updated January 15, 2021, https://biologydictionary.net/punctuated-equilibrium/. The original term used by Eldredge and Gould was the plural, "punctuated equilibria." This is actually more precise because the equilibrium shifts over time, producing multiple equilibria. However, "punctuated equilibrium" is the term that has become entrenched in the literature.

2 Tracy V. Wilson, "What if the Chicxulub Meteor Had Missed the Earth?" HowStuffWorks, September 15, 2008, https://science.howstuffworks.com/ environmental/earth/geology/chicxulub-meteor.htm.

3 Tom Flanagan, *Harper's Team: Behind the Scenes in the Conservative Rise to Power* (Montreal and Kingston: McGill-Queen's University Press, 2007), 244–45.

4 "Conservative Leader Erin O'Toole Unveils His Contrat avec les Qué- bécois et les Québécoises," Conservative Party of Canada, August 18, 2021, https://www.conservative.ca/conservative-leader-erin-otoole -unveils-his-contrat-avec-les-quebecois-et-les-quebecoises.

5 Jacob Serebrin, "Legault Says Minority Government Better for Quebec, Calls NDP, Liberals 'Dangerous,'" *CTV News,* September 9, 2021, https:// montreal.ctvnews.ca/legault-says-minority-government-better-for -quebec-calls-ndp-liberals-dangerous-1.5578691.

6 Quoted in Tom Flanagan, *Waiting for the Wave: The Reform Party and Preston Manning* (Toronto: Stoddart, 1995), 23.

7 Dave Naylor, "Wexit Canada Officially Changes Name to Maverick Party," *Western Standard,* September 17, 2020, https://www.westernstandard

online.com/2020/09/exclusive-wexit-canada officially-changes-name -to-maverick-party/.

8 Tom Flanagan, *Winning Power: Canadian Campaigning in the Twenty-First Century* (Montreal and Kingston: McGill-Queen's University Press, 2014), 49.

9 Anthony Downs, *An Economic Theory of Democracy* (New York: Harper and Row, 1957).

10 *Macbeth*, Act 5, Scene 5, ll. 27–28.

11 The model was first developed by Steven J. Brams, *Rational Politics: Decisions, Games, and Strategy* (Boston: Harcourt Brace Jovanovich, 1985), 32–36. It was applied to Canadian politics by Réjean Landry, "Incentives Created by the Institutions of Representative Democracy," in *Representation, Integration and Political Parties in Canada,* edited by Harman Bakvis (Toronto: Dundurn, 1991), 446–48.

12 Flanagan, *Waiting for the Wave,* 10.

13 Gloria Galloway and Brian Laghi, "Tories Urged to Embrace Mainstream," *Globe and Mail,* March 18, 2005, https://www.theglobeandmail.com/news/ national/tories-urged-to-embrace-mainstream/article20420610/.

14 David Dodge and Richard Dion, "Review of Economic Performance and Policy during the Harper Years," in *The Harper Factor: Assessing a Prime Minister's Policy Legacy,* edited by Jennifer Ditchburn and Graham Fox (Montreal and Kingston: McGill-Queen's University Press, 2016), ch. 8.

15 "Canada Government Debt: 2021 Data – 2022 Forecast," Trading Economics, https://tradingeconomics.com/canada/government-debt#:~: text=In%20the%20long-term%2C%20the%20Canada%20Government %20Debt%20is,government%20bond%20yields%2C%20stock%20 indexes%20and%20commodity%20prices.

16 "Canada: Gross Domestic Product (GDP) in Current Prices from 1987 to 2027," Statista, May 6, 2022, https://www.statista.com/statistics/263574/ gross-domestic-product-gdp-in-canada/.

17 Livio Di Matteo, *A Federal Fiscal History: Canada, 1867–2017* (Vancouver: Fraser Institute, 2017), 59, Table 25B, https://www.fraserinstitute.org/ sites/default/files/federal-fiscal-history-canada-1867-2017.pdf.

18 The federal Liberals led by Jean Chrétien did not support the Meech Lake Accord, but they did support the Charlottetown Accord in the end.

19 David Usborne, "Canada Reels over Quebec Revelation," *Independent,* May 12, 1997, https://www.independent.co.uk/news/world/canada-reels -over-quebec-revelation-1261120.html.

20 Hugh Winsor, "'First Nations' Fight for Freedom," *Independent,* October 6, 1995, https://www.independent.co.uk/news/world/first-nations-fight-for-freedom-1576352.html.

21 Canadian Press, "Jacques Parizeau, Former Quebec Premier and Sovereigntist Leader, Dead at 84," *National Post,* June 2, 2015, https://national post.com/news/politics/jacques-parizeau-former-quebec-premier-and-sovereigntist-leader-dead-at-84.

22 *An Act to give effect to the requirement for clarity as set out in the opinion of the Supreme Court of Canada in the Quebec Secession Reference,* SC 2000, c 26.

23 Tenille Bonoguore, "PM: Quebec 'a Nation within a United Canada,'" *Globe and Mail,* November 22, 2006, https://www.theglobeandmail.com/news/national/pm-quebec-a-nation-within-a-united-canada/article1108117.

24 Thomas Flanagan, *Game Theory and Canadian Politics* (Toronto: University of Toronto Press, 1998), 93–104.

25 "Supreme Court of Canada Appointment Process – 2019 (Appointment of the Honourable Nicholas Kasirer)," Office of the Commissioner for Federal Judicial Affairs Canada, https://www.fja-cmf.gc.ca/scc-csc/2019/index-eng.html.

26 "Canada–Québec Accord Relating to Immigration and Temporary Admission of Aliens," Government of Canada, February 5, 1991, https://www.canada.ca/en/immigration-refugees-citizenship/corporate/mandate/policies-operational-instructions-agreements/agreements/federal-provincial-territorial/quebec/canada-quebec-accord-relating-immigration-temporary-admission-aliens.html.

27 Glen Kobussen, Suresh Kalagnanam, and Whitney Loerzel, "Why Canada's Equalization Program Needs a Major Overhaul," *National Newswatch,* March 28, 2020, https://www.nationalnewswatch.com/2020/03/28/why-canadas-equalization-program-needs-a-major-overhaul/#.XoPMTkBFyUm.

28 At the provincial level, where the electorate is smaller and more homogeneous, new parties have often succeeded in forming governments: Social Credit in Alberta and British Columbia, the CCF and the Saskatchewan Party in Saskatchewan, the Progressives and CCF in Manitoba, and the Union Nationale and the Parti Québécois in Quebec, to name a few examples.

Suggestions for Further Reading

Theoretical Foundations

Rational choice, with its variants public choice and social choice, is the application of economic reasoning to the study of politics and society. It assumes that self-interest is an important determinant of human behaviour, even in areas where there is no marketplace with explicit prices. A widely read introduction for political scientists is Kenneth A. Shepsle, *Analyzing Politics: Rationality, Behavior, and Institutions*, 2nd ed. (New York: W.W. Norton, 2010).

An important part of rational choice is game theory, which provides models of interaction among two or more actors. It was first systematically expounded by the mathematical genius John von Neumann and his economist collaborator Oskar Morgenstern in 1944 in *Theory of Games and Economic Behavior*. A popularization published in 1991 and still widely read is Avinash K. Dixit and Barry J. Nalebuff, *Thinking Strategically: The Competitive Edge in Business Politics, and Everyday Life* (New York: W.W. Norton, 1991). The game-theoretical literature on Canadian politics is not very large apart from my own book, *Game Theory and Canadian Politics* (Toronto: University of Toronto Press, 1998).

The main application of game theory and rational choice in this book is coalition theory, which grew out of the analysis of cooperative n-person games. These are models of situations with more than two actors, in which the participants are allowed to form alliances to dominate those who are excluded from the winning coalition. An early application to politics was made by Anthony Downs in *An Economic Theory of Democracy* (New York:

Harper Collins, 1957), which showed the importance of the median voter, a term that has entered the vocabulary of political analysis even at a popular level.

Even more important for this book is William H. Riker, *The Theory of Political Coalitions* (New Haven, CT: Yale University Press, 1962), which emphasized the importance of the Minimum Winning Coalition (MWC). Riker showed with historical examples how coalitions larger than MWC tend to break apart, which is what happened to Brian Mulroney's Progressive Conservative coalition in 1993. An important addition to the theory of coalitions was made by Robert Axelrod, who is best known for his pioneering study of the Prisoner's Dilemma in *The Evolution of Cooperation* (New York: Basic Books, 1984). But for the purposes of this book, Axelrod's *Conflict of Interest: A Theory of Divergent Goals with Applications to Politics* (Chicago: Markham, 1970), which elaborated the concept of a Minimum Connected Winning Coalition (MCWC), is more relevant. It showed how coalitions that are internally heterogeneous, that is, marked by conflicts of interest, tend to be unstable even if they have MWC size. Axelrod's analysis helps to explain how Mulroney's coalition, which was riven with many conflicts between Quebec and the West, eventually came apart.

Primatology

Rational-choice coalition theory is bolstered by findings from the science of primatology, which has learned how members of primate species, including human beings, form coalitions to advance their interests. The seminal work is Frans de Waal's doctoral dissertation, *Chimpanzee Politics: Power and Sex among Apes* (Baltimore: Johns Hopkins University Press, 1982), based on painstaking observation of chimpanzees in the Arnhem zoo in the Netherlands. De Waal found that adult male chimpanzees form coalitions to obtain higher rank, with the result of getting preferential access to mature females in estrus, and suggested that these coalitions can be interpreted in human political terms such as rank and strategy. Study of other primate species, such as bonobos, has led to a more nuanced view, including a greater role for females in politics; see de Waal, *Bonobo: The Forgotten Ape* (Berkeley: University of California Press, 1997).

Today de Waal is probably the world's leading primatologist, though perhaps less known to the broad public than Jane Goodall, who discovered in the 1970s that chimpanzee bands in their natural setting sometimes wage a kind of low-intensity but lethal warfare against each other. Her painful discovery is described in her book *Through a Window: My Thirty Years with the Chimpanzees of Gombe* (New York: Houghton Mifflin Harcourt, 2010). Following Goodall's discovery, social scientists increasingly interpret human warfare against the backdrop of coalition formation and conflict in other primate species; see Malcolm Potts and Thomas Hayden, *Sex and War: How Biology Explains Warfare and Terrorism and Offers a Path to a Safer World* (Dallas: BenBella Books, 2008). Fortunately, we don't have to go down that bloody path in this book. For a more benign view, see Nicholas A. Christakis, *Blueprint: The Evolutionary Origins of a Good Society* (New York: Little, Brown Spark, 2019), and Mark W. Moffett, *The Human Swarm: How Our Societies Arise, Thrive, and Fall* (New York: Basic Books, 2019).

Campaigning

Political campaigning can be seen as a kind of civilized warfare, as I argued in 2013 in *Winning Power: Canadian Campaigning in the Twenty-First Century* (Montreal and Kingston: McGill-Queen's University Press, 2014). Beginning in 1984, Carleton University Press, and later Dundurn Press, has published an edited volume on each election under the title *The Canadian General Election of [election year]*. I made extensive use of the 1993 volume in preparing this book (Alan Frizzell, Jon H. Pammett, and Anthony Westell, eds., *The Canadian General Election of 1993* [Ottawa: Carleton University Press, 1994]). A recent historical synthesis of the literature on Canadian elections is Lawrence LeDuc and Jon H. Pammett, *Dynasties and Interludes: Past and Present in Canadian Electoral Politics,* 2nd ed. (Toronto: Dundurn, 2016). The most recent study of Canadian campaigning is Alex Marland and Thierry Giasson, eds., *Inside the Campaign: Managing Elections in Canada* (Vancouver: UBC Press, 2020), with contributions by participants in and observers of the 2019 general election.

Elections Canada is the official custodian of federal election results, but data from 1993 and earlier are not on its website, https://elections.ca/content. aspx?section=ele&dir=pas&document=index&lang=e. Financial data from 1993 are also not on the website but can be found in an Election Canada printed volume, *Thirty-Fifth General Election, 1993: Contributions and Expenses of Registered Political Parties* (Ottawa: Chief Electoral Officer of Canada, 1993).

Liberal Party of Canada

The Liberal Party of Canada has dominated Canadian politics since 1896, and it has received correspondingly extensive treatment by academics. A recent historical overview is R. Kenneth Carty, *Big Tent Politics: The Liberal Party's Long Mastery of Canada's Public Life* (Vancouver: UBC Press, 2015). Another informative book is Stephen Clarkson, *The Big Red Machine: How the Liberal Party Dominates Canadian Politics* (Vancouver: UBC Press, 2005).

Brooke Jeffrey, *Divided Loyalties: The Liberal Party of Canada, 1984–2008* (Toronto: University of Toronto Press, 2010), focuses on internal factionalism within the party. Because the party often seemed to have a lock on government, internal struggles have been an enticing path towards achieving power. Jeffrey's more recent book, *Road to Redemption: The Liberal Party of Canada 2006–2019* (Toronto: University of Toronto Press, 2021), chronicles the party's comeback. Susan Delacourt's book *Juggernaut: Paul Martin's Campaign for Chrétien's Crown* (Toronto: McClelland and Stewart, 2003) tells the detailed story of one episode in these long-lasting struggles. Unfortunately for Martin, the prize slipped away almost as soon as he grasped it.

Jean Chrétien is the author of three autobiographical books: *Straight from the Heart* (Toronto: Key Porter, 1985), *My Years as Prime Minister* (Toronto: Knopf Canada, 2007), and *My Stories, My Times* (Toronto: Penguin Random House, 2018). Chrétien, who would be the first to admit he's not a natural author, benefited greatly from collaboration with the journalist Ron Graham in writing the first two books. The second is even subtitled "A Ron Graham Book." Another journalist, Lawrence Martin, wrote a two-volume biography of Chrétien: *Chrétien: The Will to Win* (Toronto: Lester, 1995), and *Iron Man: The Defiant Reign of Jean Chrétien* (Toronto: Viking Canada, 2003). Unique insight into Chrétien's years as prime minister comes from his senior policy adviser Eddie Goldenberg, *The Way It Works: Inside Ottawa* (Toronto: McClelland and Stewart, 2007).

Progressive Conservative Party of Canada

The Progressive Conservatives have not elicited as much interest as the Liberals from scholars and journalists. The literature that exists consists mainly of biographies and autobiographies of leading figures in the party rather than studies of the party itself. An overview from 1993 onward is provided in J.P. Lewis and Joanna Everitt, eds., *The Blueprint: Conservative Parties and Their Impact on Canadian Politics* (Toronto: University of Toronto Press, 2017).

Brian Mulroney, of course, is an important focus. Before the 1984 election, he published *Where I Stand* (Toronto: McClelland and Stewart, 1983), meant to be a sort of election manifesto. Later, he released his lengthy *Memoirs: 1939–1993* (Toronto: McClelland and Stewart, 2007) (1,152 pages). Also worthy of note is Peter C. Newman, *The Secret Mulroney Tapes: Unguarded Confessions of a Prime Minister* (Toronto: Random House Canada, 2005), which reveals a grandiose and melodramatic personality. L. Ian MacDonald, *The Making of the Prime Minister* (Toronto: McClelland and Stewart, 1984), is a good account of Mulroney's rise to power. David J. Bercuson, J.L. Granatstein, and W.R. Young, *Sacred Trust: Brian Mulroney and the Conservative Party in Power* (Toronto: Doubleday, 1987), covers the early part of Mulroney's first term in office. A couple of scholarly books are Raymond B. Blake, ed., *Transforming the Nation: Canada and Brian Mulroney* (Montreal and Kingston: McGill-Queen's University Press, 2007), and Fen Osler Hampson, *Master of Persuasion: Brian Mulroney's Global Legacy* (Toronto: McClelland and Stewart, 2018). Among the hostile works on Mulroney, one might mention Stevie Cameron, *On the Take: Crime, Corruption and Greed in the Mulroney Years* (Toronto: Macfarlane Walter and Ross, 1994), and Harvey Cashore, *The Truth Shows Up* (Toronto: Key Porter, 2010).

Kim Campbell's autobiography, *Time and Chance: The Political Memoirs of Canada's First Woman Prime Minister* (Toronto: Doubleday Canada, 1996), explores what went wrong in 1993. Even better in that regard is *Poisoned Chalice: The Last Campaign of the Progressive Conservative Party?* (Toronto: Dundurn, 1994). Written by David McLaughlin, who worked on Campbell's campaign, it's an extremely detailed and shrewd account, which was invaluable to me in preparing this book.

Widely regarded as a classic study of a Canadian election campaign is *Letting the People Decide,* by Richard Johnston et al., which dissected the 1988 general election. An entertaining and insightful journalistic book on the same topic is by Graham Fraser, *Playing for Keeps* (Toronto: McClelland and Stewart, 1989). Preston Manning asked his aides to read Fraser's book in preparation for the 1993 election. Years later Stephen Harper appointed Fraser Commissioner of Official Languages, which was a gain to government but a loss to journalism.

There was an avalanche of writing about the constitutional struggles surrounding the Meech Lake and Charlottetown Accords. Richard Johnston, André Blais, Elisabeth Gidengil, and Neil Nevitte, *The Challenge of Direct Democracy: The 1992 Canadian Referendum* (Montreal and Kingston: McGill-Queen's University Press, 1996), is the definitive study of voting in the referendum. A list of more legally oriented works would include Patrick J. Monahan, *Meech Lake: The Inside Story* (Toronto: University of Toronto Press, 1991); Kenneth McRoberts and Patrick J. Monahan, eds., *The Charlottetown*

Accord, the Referendum, and the Future of Canada (Toronto: University of Toronto Press, 1993); and Peter Russell, *Constitutional Odyssey: Can Canadians Become a Sovereign People?* 3rd ed. (Toronto: University of Toronto Press, 2004), among others.

Reform Party of Canada/Canadian Alliance/ Conservative Party of Canada

Preston Manning is the author of two books containing both autobiography and a history of the Reform Party: *The New Canada* (Toronto: Macmillan Canada, 1992) and *Think Big: My Life in Politics* (Toronto: McClelland and Stewart, 2003). Indispensable for study of the early history of Reform is Ted Byfield, ed., *Act of Faith* (Vancouver: British Columbia Report Books, 1991), an illustrated compilation of articles from *Alberta Report, B.C. Report,* and associated magazines. Although Stephen Harper played a central role in Reform, the Canadian Alliance, and the reconstituted Conservative Party, his book *Right Here, Right Now: Politics and Leadership in the Age of Disruption* (Toronto: Penguin Random House, 2018) is a work of contemporary political analysis and doesn't deal with the history of these parties.

Sydney Sharpe and Don Braid, *Storming Babylon: Preston Manning and the Rise of the Reform Party* (Toronto: Key Porter, 1992) is an informative early account written by outsiders. For an inside view, I can mention my own books: *Waiting for the Wave: The Reform Party and Preston Manning* (Toronto: Stoddart, 1995), and *Harper's Team: Behind the Scenes in the Conservative Rise to Power* (Montreal and Kingston: McGill-Queen's University Press, 2007). The second edition of *Waiting for the Wave* (Montreal and Kingston: McGill-Queen's University Press, 2009) has additional material on the Canadian Alliance. The religious side of Manning and Harper can be difficult for secular observers to grasp. The best explanation is given by Lloyd Mackey in his books *Like Father, Like Son: Ernest Manning and Preston Manning* (Toronto: ECW Press, 1997), and *The Pilgrimage of Stephen Harper* (Toronto: ECW Press, 2005).

The most complete biography of Harper is John Ibbitson, *Stephen Harper* (Toronto: Random House, 2015). William Johnson, *Stephen Harper and the Future of Canada* (Toronto: Random House, 2005) is also very good but ends before Harper came to power. Ian Brodie, *At the Centre of Government: The Prime Minister and the Limits on Political Power* (Montreal and Kingston: McGill-Queen's University Press, 2018) has a wider focus but also says quite a bit about the Conservative government (Brodie was Harper's first chief of staff after he became prime minister). *Conservatism in Canada,* edited by James Farney and David Rayside (Toronto: University of Toronto Press, 2013), has some useful contributions. *The Harper Factor: Assessing a Prime Minister's Policy Legacy,* edited by Jennifer Ditchburn and Graham Fox (Montreal and Kingston: McGill-Queen's University Press, 2016), contains essays on multiple topics by academic and journalistic authors.

There is also no shortage of hostile books. To mention three: Marci McDonald, *The Armageddon Factor: The Rise of Christian Nationalism in Canada* (Toronto: Random House, 2010), attributes far too much importance to a tiny sliver of Conservative support. Lawrence Martin, *Harperland: The Politics of Control* (Toronto: Penguin Canada, 2011) is by a prominent *Globe and Mail* columnist. Donald Gutstein, *Harperism: How Stephen Harper and His Think Tank Colleagues Have Transformed Canada* (Toronto: James Lorimer, 2014) is a lively critique from the progressive-left wing of politics.

New Democratic Party

There is an enormous body of literature, going back to the 1930s, about the NDP and its predecessor party, the Co-operative Commonwealth Federation (CCF). Curiously, Ed Broadbent has never written an autobiography or a book about himself, even though he holds a PhD in political science. A biography by Judy Steed is titled *Ed Broadbent: The Pursuit of Power* (Markham, ON: Viking, 1988). Audrey McLaughlin published her autobiography, *A Woman's Place: My Life and Politics* (Toronto: McFarlane Walter and Ross, 1992), as a way of introducing herself to voters. The political scientist Keith Archer has written two analytical books about the NDP organization: *Political Choices and Electoral Consequences: A Study of Organized Labour and the New Democratic Party* (Montreal and Kingston: McGill-Queen's University Press, 1990), and *Political Activists: The NDP in Convention,* co-written with Alan Whitehorn (Toronto: Oxford University Press, 1998). A useful book for understanding what happened to the NDP in 1993 is *Under Siege: The Federal NDP in the Nineties* (Toronto: James Lorimer, 1994), by Ian McLeod, a party insider. I have drawn heavily upon it in my description of the NDP campaign.

Fast-forward almost two decades – in 2011, the year of the NDP's greatest success, Jack Layton published *Speaking Out Louder: Ideas That Work for Canadians* (Toronto: McClelland and Stewart, 2011). Insider Brad Lavigne wrote about that success in *Building the Orange Wave: The Inside Story behind the Historic Rise of Jack Layton and the NDP* (Madeira Park, BC: Douglas and

McIntyre, 2013). Most recently, one should consult David McGrane, *The New NDP: Moderation, Modernization, and Political Marketing* (Vancouver: UBC Press, 2019), which won the 2020 Smiley Prize sponsored by the Canadian Political Science Association.

Bloc Québécois

Lucien Bouchard published an autobiography titled À *visage découvert* (Montreal: Boreal, 1992). It was translated into English by Dominque Clift with the title *On the Record* (Toronto: Stoddart, 1994). Lawrence Martin wrote a hostile but informative biography, *The Antagonist: Lucien Bouchard and the Politics of Delusion* (Toronto: Viking, 1997). One can also consult Manon Cornellier, *The Bloc* (Toronto: J. Lorimer, 1995). There are, of course, further works in French for readers who may want to plunge more deeply into Quebec politics.

Index

Note: Page numbers with (t) refer to tables; pages with (f) refer to figures.

Meech Lake Accord, 35
See also Atlantic provinces
Newman, Peter C., 71, 168, 198
Northwest Territories
election (1988, 1993), 2(f)
election (1993), 2(f), 96(t), 97–
100, 97(t)
Nova Scotia
Charlottetown Accord, 46–48,
47(t)
election (1988, 1993), 2(f), 3–8,
4(t)
election (1993), 2(f), 96(t), 97–
100, 97(t)
See also Atlantic provinces

Ontario
Charlottetown Accord, 46–48,
47(t)
provincial PCs and merger with
Reform, 118
Rae's NDP government, 63, 100
urban-rural divide, 48, 99, 100
Ontario, general elections
election (1988, 1993), 2(f), 3–8,
4(t)
election (1993), 2(f), 96(t), 97–
100, 97(t), 113–14, 144–45
election (2011, 2015), 138
Liberals, 113–14
Reform, 144–45
urban-rural divide, 99, 100
vote splitting, 113–14
Orchard, David, 123, 168
O'Toole, Erin, 136–37, 152–53,
168

Pammett, Jon H., 102–3, 196
pandemic, COVID-19, 139, 146,
153, 156
Pantazopoulos, Dimitri, 61, 168
Parizeau, Jacques
Charlottetown Accord, 45
election (1993), 65–66
PQ premier (1994–96), 127–28,
168
referendum (1995), 9, 127–28,
148–49
Parliament. *See* House of Commons;
Senate reform policies
Parti Québécois (PQ)
Charlottetown Accord, 45
election (1993), BQ support, 66
Lévesque's leadership, 20, 85, 148,
165
Parizeau's leadership, 127–28, 168
as provincial party, 192n28
separatism, 19–20, 85, 148
sovereignty referendum (1995), 9
party system, 133–34
See also political parties; political
parties, minor; political parties,
new
PC. *See* Progressive Conservative
Party (PC) (1942–2003)
Pearson, Lester, 17, 63, 66, 168
People's Party of Canada (PPC),
138–39, 144, 156, 158
pirouette vs. pivot election (1993),
xvii–xviii, 10, 111–12, 135
pivotal median voter, 139–42
See also median voter
Poilievre, Pierre, 137, 168

Waters, Stan, 32–33
Wayne, Elsie, 99
Wells, Clyde, 35, 171
Western provinces
  about, 135–36
  Charlottetown Accord, 44–45,
    48–49
  election (1993), 106–7, 144
  Mulroney's grand coalition, 23–
    25, 37–38, 106
  political spectrum, 14–15, 27–28,
    138, 144
  realigning elections, 101–2
  Reform party, 7–8, 27–28, 41, 83,
    100, 112, 117–18, 138
  urban-rural divide, 48, 99
  views on Quebec, 44–45
  voters' shifts, 100
  Wexit/Maverick Party, 138, 163
  See also Alberta; British Colum-
    bia; Manitoba; Saskatchewan
Wexit/Maverick Party, 138, 163
White, Bob, 62–63, 171
Wildrose Party, 59
Wilson, Michael, 24, 49, 171

winning coalitions, 14–15, 21–22,
  139–40, 194–95
  See also coalition theory
women politicians
  Campbell as first prime minister
    and Conservative leader, xv, xvi,
    52, 91
  Copps as deputy prime minister,
    66–67
  gender in politics, 94
  Liberal candidates (1993), 67–68
  McDonough's NDP leadership,
    129–30, 167
  McLaughlin as first NDP leader,
    xv, xvi, 5, 52
  NDP candidates (1993), 91
  See also Campbell, Kim;
    McLaughlin, Audrey

Yukon Territory
  election (1988, 1993), 2(f)
  election (1993), 2(f), 96(t), 97–
    100, 97(t)
  McLaughlin as NDP leader, 5, 63–
    64, 97, 99–100, 167

Printed and bound in Canada by Friesens
Set in Zurich Condensed and Minion by Artegraphica Design Co.
Copy editor: Francis Chow
Proofreader: Kristy Lynn Hankewitz
Indexer: Judy Dunlop
Cartographer: Eric Leinberger
Cover designer: Will Brown